SURVIVOR

SURVIVOR

Memoir of Defeat and Captivity
Bataan, 1942

Thomas R. Harrison

Tom —
Zentsuji was
good for all of us.
The memories will
last forever —
Tom Harrison

ISBN 0-916095-29-0

Distribution by
Western Epics, Inc.
254 South Main
Salt Lake City, Utah 84101

Table of Contents

Foreword

An old truism occurs to me, that history is always written by the victors. A corollary of this is that its writers concentrate on the macro events: decisions made in high places, the movements of armies and fleets as though they were pawns on a chess board, erudite discussions of the political and economic factors that precede great conflicts and analyses of their results. The painting of the picture is done with a very broad brush and the human aspects of those events become obscured. Perhaps this is necessary. There seems to be little time or space to devote to the pilot going to a lonely death in his burning plane, the infantryman who has just been eviscerated by a fragment of shrapnel or the nurse struggling against pain and suffering in a field hospital somewhere in the jungle. They become numbers. Their sacrifices seem to be taken for granted, unfortunate but essential to the accomplishment of whatever goals have been established by the commanders. These men and women are the kind of people who make the history that others write, and they give substance to the legends that are created about the great leaders, military and political, whose names are household words. Who remembers Tom Sappington, the fifteen-year old drummer boy who fought with the Army of the South and was wounded and captured at Gettysburg? I do, because he was my grandfather, but his name will appear in none of the histories. Nor will mine in the volumes on World War II.

This book is about some of those forgotten fighters, who did what they had to do because they believed in it and because they were there. Their name is legion and they were seen across the face of the globe wherever America's battles were being waged: on the beach at Anzio, in the Bulge, in the jungles of Guadalcanal, over the Burma Road and on the ships that guarded the sea lanes to those far-flung places. My particular group was in the Philippine Islands. We came from all across this great land of ours, large cities and small, country towns and ghettos, farms and factories. We were white, brown, black and red. Some were saints and others rascals but most somewhere in between. The ancestors of some were on the shore to greet the Mayflower, others were first or second generation immigrants, but all had one thing in common—we were Americans. Our obligation to defend our country and our pride in doing it was an important part of that heritage. The fact that we were not successful in our defense did little to mitigate that pride.

This failure brings me to mid-September, 1945 when our train pulled into the Yokohama railroad station. We were greeted by brass bands playing, troops in formation with helmets and polished boots gleaming in the sun and standing at a rigid "present arms." Generals Eichelberger and Krueger saluted or shook hands with each of us as we disembarked. It was a very impressive ceremony that marked the end of the three and a half years of frustration, illness and bitterness we had experienced as unwilling guests of the Japanese people. The Americans who greeted us were well aware of our pent-up vengeful feelings toward our captors and our resolve to retaliate—physically, if possible. They prevented this by simply transferring us immediately from the railroad station to the ship which was to take us on the first leg of our journey home.

The voyage, from Japan to the Philippine Islands and thence to San Francisco, gave me time to reflect on the previous few years and the effect they had had on me, both physically and psychologically. I weighed ninety-five pounds at war's end and was twenty-seven years old, but felt much older. I was angry and resentful toward the Japanese and knew my attitude could be ruinous to me if it continued. Therefore, I made up my mind to put the war period behind me, and to begin the rest of my life unencumbered by the rage and hatred that had been a part of me for so long. As a part of that therapy, for many years I have refused to dwell on or to discuss those times in any detail with anyone, excepting for an anecdote from time to time. The resolution has been partially successful.

My wife, daughter and two sons have always been curious about those experiences but reluctant to insist on the telling of them for fear of re-opening old wounds. It is, however, a part of their birthright and this book is an attempt to relieve their curiosity. To begin it with the surrender of Bataan and the starting of the "Death March" would not be appropriate. There would be no understanding of the events, both intimate and military, which led to those disasters, and no insight into the maturation process that took place in their husband and father along the way.

My story is a personal chronicle covering the period beginning with induction into the Service in 1941 and ending with return to the United States in 1945. It does not contain a scholarly historical analysis of grand strategy and military tactics, but concerns my limited understanding of that strategy and those tactics at the time they occurred, and as they affected me individually. In short, this letter to my family recounts the day to day experiences of one very minor segment of a much larger picture. With changes in detail only, it could be retold by any of the other thousands who comprised the USAFFE, and, more particularly, the USFIP. It is dedicated to the ones still living and to the memory of those who did not survive.

Acknowledgments

This book could not have been written without the encouragement and assistance freely given by others. The inspiration to begin, and the motivation to continue through long hours at the computer, came from my dear wife, Dorothy. My daughter Jane contributed many suggestions that helped me to establish format, to develop a readable presentation and to avoid many of the traps that could have weakened it. The final editing task fell to my daughter-in-law, Ann. It was meticulously done, with dispatch and at some personal sacrifice, and I shall always be grateful.

I showed early drafts to comrades who had shared many of the experiences with me: Chuck Francis, Kermit Lay and Bill Smith. Their comments were most valuable in correcting errors of fact, and provided insights that strengthened the book. Bill Smith permitted the use of the sketches of prison camp life he had collected, and which add so much. Some of the photographs came from Jack Gates, who was at Zentsuji and Rokuroshi with me. The maps of Luzon and Bataan were extracted from an excellent volume, "The Second World War", a part of the West Point Military History Series. Information on the

British 75-millimeter cannon was furnished by the U. S. Army Field Artillery & Fort Sill Museum at Fort Sill, Oklahoma. There are many others who assisted me in many ways—thank you all.

1

The Beginning

In early June of 1941, the University of Utah graduating class assembled in Kingsbury Hall for the awarding of degrees and conferring of such honors as the members of the senior class had been able to garner during their years on campus. It was a small group; the entire student body at that time comprised only thirty-nine hundred people. Some of the ones on stage that day were not there to receive degrees, but to be commissioned as Second Lieutenants in the Army of the United States. Degrees, when earned, would come later. I was one of those. The kicker was that, along with the commission, each of us were handed a set of Orders (always capitalized) authorizing us to proceed to Camp Roberts, California for training. We would subsequently be assigned to one of the US Army units being formed and expanded to meet the confrontation with Germany (and possibly Japan) that was clearly going to occur in the near future. Among the first to be inducted into the Service, we were part of a trickle which became a flood very shortly thereafter.

There were no options; we had spent the previous few years in the Reserve Officers Training Corps (ROTC), and were supposedly qualified to lead soldiers into battle or wherever. Furthermore, the commission carried with it an obligation to serve when called. I had always been intrigued by things military and had entered the ROTC while in high school. I continued it enthusiastically through an otherwise undistinguished college career, so the Orders to active duty were not unwelcome. All I had to do was pass a physical exam—not difficult for a young buck of twenty-two—and I was in.

After the indignities of that physical at Fort Douglas were over: the punctures, the probes, the X-Rays, primitive though they were in those days, spatula down the throat, "say AH!," examine for existing scars, a peek into the orifices, etcetera, I was certified as able to withstand the rigors of military life. The next step was to proceed to the first duty assignment, pursuant to the thirteen sets of Orders which were required for all transient personnel to carry at all times.

So I set off with Bob Patterson and Harold Linke in Bob's little Willys coupe. All our worldly goods were packed in the trunk, on the top, behind the seat and anywhere else they could be tied or taped or otherwise secured. We had been fraternity brothers while at the University and were good friends. Harold was an engineer, tall, blonde and serious-minded. Bob was a geologist who had been brought up around horses and loved them, which is probably the reason he was ultimately assigned to the pack artillery in the South Pacific. Automobile air-conditioning had not yet been well developed and the trip was uncomfortable. It was then late June and very hot across the desert, with a brief respite when we went over Donner Pass, then more heat as we traveled down the central valley of California to Camp Roberts.

To describe that place adequately is difficult. It was located about fifteen miles inland from the Pacific coastline, south of Salinas and a few miles north of Atascadero. The Coast Range of mountains separated it from the ocean, and also from the cool breezes that make the beaches so pleasant. The hot winds and blazing sun combined to make the touching of any exposed surface an unwelcome adventure. Some committee had spent much time and taxpayers' money trying to find an area absolutely valueless for any other purpose and with no redeeming features at all, for siting this camp. They had succeeded admirably. There was, literally, only one tree on the whole Post, on the hill in front of the Headquarters Building. The rest was manzanita, cactus (the low-lying kind that traps the unwary) and very sparse grass, brown and crackly underfoot at that time of year. The foothills to the west were cut by sharp arroyos in the sandy soil which then fanned out into a narrow valley, the only flat place around, and in which the post buildings were located.

Camp Roberts was intended to be a Replacement Depot, where men were inducted into the Army and given basic training before being assigned to specific units elsewhere. It was a complex of new wooden barracks, two-story with open bunking areas, private NCO quarters and common latrine/shower rooms. Each was exactly like every other, and they were connected together by wood duck-board walkways. These were for the trainees. The officers fared better. Our quarters had the same appearance externally, but were divided inside into small cubicles, each accommodating two men with all their gear. Furnishings consisted of two military cots, two chairs, two small desks, linoleum floor covering, one bare light bulb hanging on a wire from the center of the ceiling and an inadequate wardrobe closet. Washroom facilities were at the end of this one-story building, utilitarian but offering no privacy whatsoever. Air conditioning was in its infancy in those days, and in any case would have been much too effete for youngsters who were about to become Army MEN.

Across the main north-south highway to the east of the camp was the East Garrison and north of that Hunter-Liggett, another poorly endowed piece of real estate. They were in the same type country, with few roads and no buildings or any other signs of human attention. Incorporated as a part of Camp Roberts, they would be used for the field exercises that formed an integral part of military training. These three areas, taken together, merited fully the hoary old expression, "If the world were to be given an enema, it would be inserted here."

We reported to Camp Headquarters, together with our thirteen copies of Orders, and were formally installed as part of the official training cadre. Our duties were to make soldiers out of country bumpkins, city slickers and various other categories in vogue at the time. Since we were neophytes ourselves, this would turn out to be no easy task. Each of us drew an assignment; mine was Motor Officer, with the responsibility of training inductees in the intricacies of operating the military vehicles then in use. They ranged from pick-up trucks through 4 x 2's, 4 x 4's, 4 x 6's and 6 x 6's. At that time, we had no Jeeps. In case this terminology is confusing, a 4 x 2 is a ton-and-a-half truck with two driven wheels, a 4 x 4 is similar with four-wheel drive, a 4 x 6 is a two-and-a-half ton vehicle having four driving wheels, and a 6 x 6 is the same size but with all-wheel drive. I was a logical choice for this teaching assignment because the only previous experience I had had was driving my father's automobile plus a couple of hours in a 4 x 2. Our college training unit had been horse-drawn artillery. To utilize such expertise was then typical of the Army Way, so it required a great deal of study and ingenuity for me to keep ahead of the training schedule. Even then I made some gross errors.

The first class I had, consisting of about forty men, had as its objective the introduction of civilians to the efficient operation of military transport. I made certain assumptions, one of them being that everybody had some experience with cars. Not so. In the opening session we used the 4 x 2 for training since other than the pickup, it was the simplest vehicle in the inventory. One by one, the trainees would get into the truck with a non-commissioned instructor, drive it around the prescribed course and back to the point of beginning, then turn it over to a successor. After about half of the group had advanced through this exercise, I ordered the next man in the series to proceed with the maneuvers, anticipating no problems. To my surprise, he refused. I repeated the order and still he refused. What to do? I had several alternatives, one of which was to court martial the man for ''Refusal to Obey a Lawful Order,'' a last resort kind of solution not really appropriate for a brand new officer on his first day of duty. Fortunately, the problem was solved without making an issue of it. A few inquiries of him revealed that he was born and reared in San Francisco, had never in his life operated a motor vehicle and had been too nervous to admit it. We modified our course after that to include the most elementary instruction in automobiles and trucks: what they could do, how it was done and why it was done. This brought our San Franciscan, plus others in like condition, up to parity with most of the rest and allowed the course to proceed to its ordained conclusion. From that incident, I learned that even in an authoritarian military organization, soldiers were people of many backgrounds and varying personalities and, excepting for mass formations, had to be treated as individuals. An officer needs to know his men and establish mutual trust with them in order to be effective as a teacher and leader. I almost blew that one.

After a week or so glorified driver training began to get old. Group after group came into the course, completed it and departed to other areas of instruction. Whatever challenge there had been became routine, and physical conditions did not improve; on the contrary, as the summer wore on the heat intensified. This was not the adventure and new experience I had envisioned. So I was ripe for the announcement that was posted on the Camp bulletin board early in July, these well-remembered words:

> "Volunteers will be accepted for duty in the
> Philippine Islands.
> Assignments will be for a minimum of two years.
> Dependents are not authorized . . ."

On the day this notice appeared, the temperature was 117 degrees fahrenheit, with no relief in sight. Small wonder that the visions of a tropical paradise, soft sea air, palm trees, scantily-clad girls and the countless other exotic attractions of an unknown area were more than appealing. It took me almost two minutes to make up my mind to try it. I marched to headquarters, announced my intentions and signed the necessary papers. It should have been a warning that none of the officers connected with Personnel advanced any objections or alternative courses of action, or attempted in any way to dissuade me. But in my state of euphoria, such cautions would have made no impression anyway. I was not alone; several of the others there had been infected with the same virus, and also ended up on the list of volunteers. Reed Shurtleff, Eugene Holmes, George Armantrout and some others from the U of U, a couple from the Missouri School of Mines, a few from Stanford, Bill Smith from Oregon State and Chuck Francis out of Santa Clara University were among them.

In a way it was like old-home week. We all knew each other, either from our days in college or from the shared experience of ROTC summer training at Camp Ord (now Fort Ord) near Monterey, California. We had lived there in tents, performed KP together in the mess hall, withstood the cold morning fogs and the baking of the afternoon sun and had fought the tough old animals of horse-drawn artillery. Putting up with hazing from the NCO's and privates of the regular Army cadre who were responsible for our teaching had forged bonds of friendship that still tie us together—at least those who survived.

It was amazing how fast the Army could act when it chose to do so. Within a week the Orders were cut and we received thirteen copies of a new set of Orders, directing us to proceed (a good Army phrase) to Fort Mason in San Francisco for overseas transportation to Manila, P.I. Bob and Harold elected to stay at Roberts. We considered it a poor decision on their part, but it may have been the best one they ever made.

2

In Transit

Reed, George and I took off for San Francisco, this time in Reed's car, planning to stop in Sacramento to visit with Reed's parents. His father was the General Manager of the Wonder Baking Company, having been transferred from the same position in Salt Lake. We had lived two doors apart on Second South St. there, and he was one of my best friends. I remember little of the trip except one episode in Sacramento. That city is the capitol of California, and there were several good inns that catered to legislators. The most outstanding was the Senate Hotel, not far from the state government complex. It had one of the few air-conditioned bars then in existence, and we went there one very hot afternoon. All of us ordered a bottle of Ranier Ale, which was so cold and good that I ordered another, against Reed's advice; I thought the day had not yet arrived when I couldn't consume two beers at one time. It was a mistake. We finished the ale and left the bar, going from air-conditioned comfort to 102 degree temperature outside. The temperature change had its effect. I fell flat on my face in the middle of the sidewalk as though I had been poleaxed, to a chorus of slurs from those I had counted as friends.

We arrived in San Francisco and reported to Fort Mason, Orders in hand, for processing out to the western

Pacific. Fort Mason was a debarkation center located on the south side of the Bay about three or four miles from the Golden Gate Bridge. It had temporary quarters for transient personnel, an elaborate clinic for physical examinations, an indoctrination center with all the services needed by those about to leave: finance, shipping of personal effects, ship assignments and so on. My first experience was a duplicate, with flourishes, of the one I had undergone at Fort Douglas. This time there were shots, given on an assembly-line basis as we shuffled in a line between two rows of corpsmen, each armed with a syringe containing different antibodies, and each more than willing to share those with us. By the time we reached the end, we had been protected against almost every known tropical ailment for at least a year or more. Needless to say, the aftermath for me was acute discomfort for a day or two. This behind me (that too had been punctured) the lectures concerning our destination and the problems we might face began. We had the VD series, the cultural orientation, the legal situation analysis, the relationship between military and native civilian and the obligations of Americans serving in a dependent country. The lectures were informative, confusing and fascinating.

Things went along very well until we arrived in the office to receive our final departure orders. Then, for a reason I still don't understand, I found that my own Orders and those of two or three more had been changed. Shurtleff, Armantrout and Holmes were to depart on the SS President Coolidge within the week. We others were instructed to report to HQ, where we were informed that we had been cancelled and should have to wait until new Orders for other destinations had been cut. I objected strongly and did what I could to reactivate the original plans. I found out later that one of the officers had a change of heart about going to the Philippines, and stated that others, including me, were similarly affected. How he got away with it I don't know, since I was never consulted. It took some days to straighten this out and in the interval the Coolidge sailed. After another few days, there were a new set of Orders available for me, destination still Manila. Departure was delayed until the sailing of the SS President Cleveland about the tenth of August, three weeks away. I was assigned TDY (temporary duty) at Fort Mason in the interim, with absolutely no duties to perform. There were quarters available on the Post at no cost, but other expenses were mine. At that time, the pay of a Second Lieutenant was $125 per month, so there wasn't much money available for sight-seeing or entertainment. Even so I managed, with the help of four partial payments against accrued salary. The Finance Officer must have thought I was nuts, asking for two or three days of that accrued pay at a time.

I had a chance to prowl the City, and enjoyed every minute of it, riding the cable cars until I had saddle sores, spending time at the Cliff House having its famous Ramos Fizzes and watching the seals cavort on the rocky islets just offshore. I sought out, in the company of a girl from Salt Lake who was stationed there with the Red Cross, the good restaurants whose prices fit my budget and looked through the museums and other landmarks of San Francisco. By the time it was over, I felt very cosmopolitan indeed.

I visited Alcatraz, the toughest federal prison in the country. It was on an island with no water wells, and the only supply came from the small water tender that made one or two trips to the island each day. I not only managed to secure a trip on that boat, but was allowed to take the wheel for a while until the Skipper noticed that our path varied much more than it should have, the wake resembling a slalom course. Steering a ship is not the easiest task in the world and I turned out to be one of the least efficient steersman they had yet discovered, but I enjoyed the experience and we reached Alcatraz unscathed. The prison itself was depressing, grey and grim. Those on the boat were not allowed ashore nor were the inmates allowed aboard, and no conversation at all was permitted between us. It was all business: hook up the hoses, pump the water, disengage and leave.

Since there was some time left before departure I thought it would be nice to go home for a few days for a visit, coincident with my twenty-third birthday, and I found there was a way to do it at no cost. Hamilton Field was located north of the Golden Gate Bridge near Sausalito. It served as a base for the Air Transport Command, using C-46 and C-47 airplanes, which became famous as the DC-2 and -3 series. I managed to hitch a ride from there to Salt Lake on one of those planes. The trip was a good interlude and also relieved the pressures on my pocketbook. Included in that visit was a garden birthday party at the home of the Friendly's, my aunt and uncle, giving me the chance to see family and friends one more time before going overseas. Some of those I was never to see again, but others are still close. Although I didn't know it at the time Jane, a girl who would later be my sister-in-law, became engaged that night to a fraternity brother, on the bridge crossing the stream behind the house. It must have been very romantic.

Good things never last however, and it was soon time to get back to Fort Mason. I did that by the same means, hitching an airplane ride to Hamilton and then taking a bus to the City. I arrived only a couple of days prior to the sailing of the President Cleveland, which was gratifying since I was financially unable to enjoy much more of San Francisco. We boarded the ship in the morning and actually left the pier late in the afternoon, passing under the Golden Gate Bridge not long before sunset. It was a beautiful evening, and the sight of the City fading into the slight haze to the east was one I will not forget. I was excited at the beginning of my great adventure and buoyed by the realization that for the first time in my life, I was truly on my own.

This trip was the first made by the Cleveland as a troop transport. It had been a cruise ship, mainly between the West Coast and Hawaii, for a number of years. The only conversion made to suit its new assignment was the installation of about forty double-decker bunks in what had been the Tea Room, at the aft end of the upper deck. My allotted space was there, and naturally, being both high and aft of the center of gravity, it got all the corkscrew motion of the ship resulting from our first meeting with the ocean swells. Even in rowboats my experience had been limited, so the rolling and pitching very quickly sent me to my bunk, an upper, of course, suffering from my first and only case of seasickness. Thankfully, it was light and of short duration, gone before morning. We were less than a week into Honolulu, where we spent a day and a night. Three new friends, Harold ''Hap'' Armold, Bob Silhavy, Gene Boyt and I took a suite in the Royal Hawaiian Hotel, then the most luxurious hostelry in the Islands. It was all we had desired until the next morning, when we were faced with an infestation of cockroaches in the bathroom. Given our previous experience, this was both unusual and disgusting, though in the years to follow such things became commonplace. Beautiful as it was, my only memory of that time in Hawaii is of those cockroaches.

The vessel was bound for Manila loaded with nearly a thousand troops, our complement of fifty or sixty ''casual,'' or unassigned, officers and twelve Army nurses bound for the General Hospital at Fort McKinley. These gals were the subject of much good-natured but lascivious girl-watching and a source of competition among our group, none of it successful; they had more experience than we. These same nurses became real heroines later, both in Bataan and on Corregidor. Hap Armold was lucky enough to marry one of them after the war. He was one of the nice guys one meets along the way: easy to know, comfortable to be around and a gentleman.

Shipboard life quickly became routine; you could walk the deck only so many times and play only so many games of shuffleboard. The ship's swimming pool was not filled, but we did do a lot of sun-bathing there because the nurses did. Frequently, I found myself either at the bow or at the stern of the ship watching the wake, particularly in the night, staring at the fluorescence in the water caused by the disturbance of our passing. From the stern, it resembled myriad small intermittent lamps that shined in the dark as if to show the course we had followed. From the bow, the glowing wave seemed a protest by the sea at having its slumber interrupted. The phenomenon was fascinating to me, and became more pronounced as we entered the southerly latitudes. Our course was southwesterly and we saw no land until we arrived at the eastern edge of the Philippine archipelago. Before the islands came into view, however, we knew we were near because of the many birds and much floating debris visible. We had seen a few flying fish as we worked further south, but now there were many of them, usually sailing through the air only a few feet above the water but occasionally getting high enough to slide across the deck. The flying fish is about a foot long, with fins projecting to each side eight inches or so. It develops high speed through the water, then launches itself into the air and skims close to the surface for sixty to eighty feet before splashing back. I never learned the purpose of this flying. It could have been to catch airborne insects or something else that was edible, just play, or an attempt to escape some larger pursuing fish.

The night before we sighted land we saw our first manta, or giant ray. It was a big one, maybe eight feet across and six feet long, with a mean-looking stinger at the tail. It had no fins, but powerful wings that extended to each side and made it appear diamond-shaped when viewed from above. This one jumped out of the water, flexed its muscles and fell back with the kind of splash I used to make when I was learning to swan dive, a demonstration of raw power that made a deep impression.

A more disturbing incident occurred about two in the morning. There was a great commotion on deck and we trooped out to find that the ship had run down a small fishing vessel. Torn in two, it sank rapidly. Our crew launched a boat immediately and, using floodlights, megaphones for giving directions, a lot of cursing and some praying, managed to rescue the fishermen before any life was lost. Thoughts of sharks and giant rays and what they could have done to those Filipinos (the first we had seen), and the expectation of landfall by early morning, kept me on deck the rest of the night.

By daylight, we were off the east coast of the islands, near the mouth of the San Bernardino Strait. There appeared to be hundreds of them, varying in size from small projections to large landmasses. All were just like the travel posters had said they would be, with white sandy beaches backed by some of the most lush, intensely green growth I had ever seen. The day was cloudless, with so little wind there was hardly a ripple on the water, and from our distance there was no visible evidence of human habitation. The islands were emerald projections rising out of a glistening sea.

We threaded our way through the strait and into the Visayan Sea, with the island of Samar to port and Luzon to starboard. These were the major ones. Many other smaller islets were on all sides. There was also much seaborne activity, fishing boats, little inter-island steamers, dug-out canoes called ''bancas,'' some of which had sails, and lateen-rigged ''praus'' typical of those used almost universally by the Moros of Mindanao.

The ship then turned north and proceeded up the west coast of Luzon through the Visayan and Sibuyan Seas, passing the Islands of Masbate, Sibuyan, Marinduque and Mindoro on our approach to Manila Bay. Our last night aboard ship was spent in this area, and in the tradition of the old cruise lines, there was a Captain's Dinner, very formal, with everyone in his best uniform and on his best behavior. It was quite a party and one of the last of its kind for the military transports. That festive civilian tradition was suspended shortly after for the duration, because the Services needed no such frivolities.

By the time we neared the entrance to Manila Bay the next morning, we had been almost surfeited by tropical beauty. Later, I learned a song of many verses, some of them clean. Its chorus, which would soon take on real meaning for all of us, went something like this:

Zamboanga! Oh, pretty Zambo
From a transport you look so swell
But before I'd serve another tour in Zambo
I would rather serve a longer tour in Hell!

Fairly early in the day, we entered Manila Bay, passing between the Bataan Peninsula to the north and the "impregnable fortress" of Corregidor to the south. Neither had much significance then, but became very important to us later. It was the twenty-eighth of August, 1941; we had been sailing for nineteen days and looked forward to setting foot on land. It took a couple of hours to transit the bay and our ship finally tied up at the dock in the Port of Manila around noon. Naturally, the Army had different ideas about our opportunities for sight-seeing than we did. The first of those was that we did not disembark until a reception detail came aboard, set up their desks and began our in-processing to the Department of the Philippines. As always, the first question asked was, "Let me see your Orders." All thirteen copies were then duly presented and separated into piles destined for the Adjutant General, the duty post to be assigned, the Medical Department, the Finance Office, the Personnel section and others whose titles and responsibilities I never did find out. With this completed, we were officially welcomed to the Islands and given the usual indoctrination lectures covering everything that could possibly happen to us while in the Department, except the one thing that did happen, war.

The casuals were divided into groups according to destination: nurses to Fort McKinley, some of the officers to the 31st Infantry stationed in Manila, some to the Coast

Artillery on Corregidor and a few to various support activities in different locations. The rest were to be sent to the Philippine Scout Artillery and Cavalry then stationed at Fort Stotsenburg in the province of Pampanga. The 200th Coast Artillery were to go as a unit to their assigned post, as were the 192nd and 194th Tank Battalions to theirs. Those three were National Guard outfits: the 200th from New Mexico, the 192nd from Wisconsin, Kentucky and Illinois and the 194th from Minnesota, Missouri and California. All were to give outstanding subsequent service.

By the time these preliminaries were completed, we felt that we would finally be able to sample the fabled attractions of Manila and begin to experience first-hand the "mystery of the Orient." Again, the Army had other ideas. They were not the least bit interested in our yearnings for romantic interludes. What the Army wanted was for us to get to work as soon as possible, and it tried its damnedest to see that we did just that. We finally left the ship, going not into sight-seeing busses but into Dodge 4 x 2 personnel carriers. All our baggage, previously loaded for us by Filipino stevedores, went with us. Thus began the trip to Fort Stotsenburg, about sixty miles, or 96 kilometers, northwesterly from Manila. It was a harrowing trip, mostly because traffic lanes were on the English system; one drove on what we considered the wrong side of the road. In addition, traffic was dense. There were carabao carts for hauling farm produce, caratellas (two-wheeled taxicabs drawn by very small undernourished horses), automobiles and foot travelers, all vying for the right of way. Mostly, the trucks won, and we arrived at Fort Stotsenburg keyed up and exhilarated, in the late afternoon.

To me, Stotsenburg was a beautiful place. It was then

the headquarters of the Philippine Scout field artillery and cavalry units, and also had as an adjunct the recently activated Clark Field Air Base. With the exception of the air base, it had been in existence since not long after the Spanish-American War of 1898. The main post consisted of a central parade ground, bordered on the south by the enlisted barracks and on the north by the officers' club and lovely old frame homes which had been allocated to officers' families. On the west end was post headquarters, flanked by the Commanding General's quarters. Behind the headquarters were the post theater and other support buildings. The east end faced on the Clark Field complex, which consisted of warehouses and command structures. Clark had an east-west runway, which was flanked by revetted parking spots for the airplanes, P-40 fighters and some of the first B-17 bombers deployed in the Pacific.

To the southwest, in the far corner, were the shops and service areas, and to the east of those were the stables for the cavalry, the field artillery gun parks, vehicle storage areas and the other working sections of the Fort. The post was liberally festooned with wonderful old mango trees about forty feet tall, whose wide-spreading branches and dark green foliage provided much-needed shade. North of the officers'quarters was the eighteen hole golf course, with well manicured grass fairways, but sand greens. More trees, mangoes and others, dotted this course and made it a very pleasant place to spend a few hours. After settling in, we did that as often as possible. The first hole was in the parade ground, with the tee directly across the street from the quarters to which we were ultimately assigned. The atmosphere was one of peace and quiet and the good life we had hoped to encounter. I loved it from the beginning.

3

Duty Station

Our convoy drove into the Fort at mid-afternoon and went directly to Headquarters where, after a brief welcoming ceremony, we were allocated quarters and given duty assignments. Shurtleff, Holmes and Armantrout had already been assigned to the 24th Field Artillery (PS). Bill Smith also went to the 24th, and the rest of the new arrivals were sent to the other battalions, including Chuck Francis and myself. I was assigned to Headquarters Battery, 88th Field Artillery (PS), and given the position of Motor Officer, in charge of all the battalion vehicles and prime movers (trucks used to pull the guns). It was an obvious choice for them to make, since I had had such intensive experience at Camp Roberts.

Fort Stotsenburg was the headquarters for the Philippine Scout (PS) cavalry and artillery units. Stationed there at that time were the 26th Cavalry and the 24th, 86th and 88th Field Artillery battalions. The Philippine Scouts were an elite organization, comprised of American officers and Filipino enlisted ranks. The Scouts had been in existence since the United States took control of the Islands from Spain. For the Filipino, membership in these units was a coveted honor. Once accepted, he could expect to spend the balance of his career as a part of the most prestigious military organization in the country. Applicants for enlistment were so numerous that realistically, very few other than the sons of active or retired soldiers could expect to be selected. For all candidates, the ability to speak English was mandatory. They set high standards for themselves, their officers and their units, and those who failed to meet these were soon eliminated. The Scouts were the only native military organization in the Philippines which was experienced enough to form training cadres for a larger Army in times of emergency. That they were not so utilized when war actually came was, I believed at the time, a major error in the defense of the islands. Instead, they were kept as a part of the Philippine Division or related units, and used as backup reserves to the Philippine Army divisions. There was one other possible cadre group, the graduates of the Philippine Military Academy, some of whom were excellent officers, but their number was small. Very young men were, of necessity, given command responsibilities far beyond their experience and maturity.

After receiving our duty assignments, we were given the opportunity to unpack and settle in. In the beginning our Orders had stated that dependents were not authorized, and all families who had been in residence at the post were gone. They had been sent back to the States, the last of them in the very ship that had brought us. Therefore, quarters that had been their homes were now available to groups of single officers. The house to which we were assigned was large, old and comfortable. It was located adjacent to the officers club on the east side of that facility, and was a two-story structure that had a screened-in porch across the front and along one side of the first floor. The high-ceilinged rooms were large and relatively cool because of the shade from trees surrounding the building. What had been a single-family home was now devoted to four Lieutenants, which, I am sure, was a source of confusion to the seven servants we had inherited, who constituted our house staff. Each of us ended up with his own room, minimally furnished with items discarded by previous occupants.

Reed, Gene, George and I shared the house. Our needs were served by two houseboys, one cook and four lavanderas. The latter were responsible for seeing that our clothes were clean and starched and that we were always presentable. This may seem a simple task until the scope of their work is understood. Our workday began at seven-thirty with the morning formation of the battalions, and continued until noon. There was an hour for lunch, and then another session from one until two-thirty in the afternoon. Since we were required to be immaculate at all times, this meant at least two, and sometimes three uniform changes a day, forced by dust, heat and sweat. Another change was required after six. All officers were expected to be in dress whites for the evening, even though there was no one left to admire this sartorial splendor excepting ourselves. I suppose one reason for these stiff uniform regulations was to maintain pride of self and to keep unattached, feisty young men from "going native." All the clothing items were washed by hand then starched and pressed with a heavy iron heated on the stove. Those lavanderas, and the other servants, really earned their very small wages, which cost each of us only thirty dollars per month, total.

We had not been able to acquire this variety of uniforms in the States, because of limited finances and equally limited information about requirements. Therefore, the first order of business after moving in to the house was to arrange for the services of the post tailor and the bootmaker. I placed a telephone call to their respective offices, requesting their presence at my quarters the following afternoon. Both arrived at the appointed time on bicycles, pencil and pad in hand, to take the necessary measurements. The tailor recorded the information he needed, and then departed with the commitment to produce three working uniforms and one set of whites within three days. The bootmaker made a tracing of my foot on a piece of brown paper, added some cabalistic numbers indicating arch location and height, and also departed with promises to deliver brown shoes and whites at the same time as the uniforms. This seemed impossible to me, but it turned out to be the first and only time in all my Philippine experience that promises, once made, were fulfilled. On the second day both of them came by the quarters for fittings, and on the third the finished articles were delivered. The khaki work uniforms consisted of shirt, tie and trousers that fit like the paper on the wall. The whites were elegant: dress trousers, white shirt, black tie and a blouse complete with gold buttons and gold braid epaulets. There was also a white dress cap with no gold braid on the visor; Second Lieutenants do not rate that distinction. There were three pairs of shoes, one white and two brown, the best fitting I had ever worn. All were oxfords (field boots could be drawn from Quartermaster stores). The cost was unbelievably low even by the depression standards I knew. Shoes were five dollars a pair and the uniforms cost ten per set, including ties. Whites were a little higher priced, but not much. Later I found out one reason the shoes were so cheap. They were made of carabao hide, which is tough and durable but has a terrible odor when wet. In this tropical climate that happened all too frequently, and those shoes were among the first things I discarded after the war began.

I remember few of my fellow officers in the battalion, but I do remember the First Sergeant of the HQ Battery, Sergeant Agpoon. He was tall for a Filipino, with graying hair and the generous build that comes from years of good living. He was fastidious about his grooming and was very professional. He had obviously seen many Second Lieutenants come and go over the years. He knew our shortcomings, and was not only able but willing to help us over the rough spots that all new men encounter on their first duty tours. As the weeks passed, he managed to help me keep functioning more or less efficiently for the entire time I was assigned to the 88th. I shall always feel indebted to him for his patience, understanding and counsel. As an example of that counseling, all new officers had to qualify as marksmen with small arms. When my turn came, Sgt. Agpoon warned me that my standing with the troops would depend on how well I did on the firing range, since they admired skill so much. Because I have always been a poor shot, this worried me, and I took particular care in preparation of the rifle and adjusting the sight. I was able to score five bulls-eyes in five shots for the first time in my life. He had been right; the men were duly impressed and it showed in their attitude and in the way they worked for me thereafter. I was smart enough not to expose myself to further trials and stayed away from the range after that.

I enjoyed serving with the Scouts. They were very spit and polish; precise at drill, uniforms immaculate and the materiel and other equipment were always well-maintained. In addition, they were trained and expert at their assignments, whether it be as gun crews, drivers, fire control men or forward observers. Because of the uneasiness in the Far East at that time, there were many field exercises. These were simulated battle situations, sometimes performed in conjunction with the infantry and sometimes by ourselves, but always very serious. They were followed by frequent performance critiques from the battalion commander and his staff. The younger reserve officers had been fairly well taught in the ROTC, but the training at Fort Stotsenburg was intensive and professional, and did a lot to sharpen our military skills.

At that time, the 88th FA was assigned as backup for the defense of the potential landing sites along the south shore of Lingayen Gulf, in the northwesterly quadrant of the island of Luzon. As one step in the familiarization process, the new officers were taken on a reconnaisance trip through this area. Our route was westerly from San Fernando, Pampanga to the coastline of the China Sea, in the province of Zambales. We then proceeded north along the coast through Iba, cut across the Lingayen Peninsula to the Gulf coast and thence east along that coastline through the towns of Lingayen and Dagupan to San Fernando, La Union. From there we headed back down the interior highway to the other San Fernando and into Stotsenburg. The trip was leisurely, with frequent stops to become familiar with local areas. It took place during our first week and helped to acquaint us with the terrain. It also provided us a glimpse of the people and the kind of life they lived: agrarian, slow-paced and seemingly carefree. That short journey revealed a way of life totally different from anything in our prior experience. We learned that, if we were to be successful with the Filipinos, we would need to adapt to their lifestyle, rather than they to ours. At one of our stops, just outside of Dagupan, we were parked alongside the road for an orientation lecture on the problems of defending a sandy, open beach area. A small woman walked by bare-footed, wearing a long skirt and loose blouse. She decided to urinate and did it, right in the middle of the dusty road, by simply spreading her feet, raising the skirt a trifle and letting go. None of the old hands paid the slightest attention, though I was startled. What had always been to me a very private function, especially for ladies, was suddenly quite public, to be done whenever and wherever the need arose without embarrassment. The incident was one small example of the many disparities between our cultures. Some of those would appear charming to the observer but could be totally frustrating to one who was required to work with them on a day to day basis.

The two and a half months I spent with the Scouts taught me a great deal, but it was not all work. Mandatory for all newly-arrived officers at any Army post is a formal call on the Commanding Officer at his quarters. This is done in the evening and dress uniform is obligatory. The first thing we did after getting our new clothing was to make the arrangements for our own visit. One did not just drop in. Protocol was to arrange a time and a date through his aide, then to be there exactly at that time. Our visit went well. The CO was then Brigadier General Edward C. King. He turned out to be as warm a personality as a General could be when entertaining Second Lieutenants. He made our brief thirty minute call both pleasant and memorable with his tales about the Scouts and their history. General King was later promoted to Major General and given command of the USFIP forces on Bataan a short while before it fell. He was to have the most disheartening task any commander could perform in surrendering them to the Japanese.

One of my major vices, then and now, is the game of golf. The opportunities for this were many. Our quarters were directly across the street from the first tee, and our normal working day ended at two-thirty in the afternoon. Even though it was very hot and humid, the combination of proximity and time available was irresistible and we played frequently. Each of the foursome had a caddy; mine carried my old canvas bag with a hole in it, containing no two clubs of the same make or style. Nonetheless, he took care of them as though they had been made of solid silver. As an ex-caddy, I revelled in that luxury. There was an additional service. In addition to the bag-carriers, we had extra caddies who had only two functions. One of these was to smooth the sand greens between the ball and the hole before we putted. The most important other duty was to run between wherever we were and the clubhouse, fetching beer and other refreshment. This entourage was sheer luxury at a daily rate of fifty cents per caddy.

As officers, we were required to learn to be experts at driving every type of vehicle assigned to our unit. Included among them were motorcycles, and after demonstrating a sufficient degree of proficiency, we were allowed to check them out for use in exploring the adjacent areas. We took full advantage, visiting San Fernando and the small barrios nearby frequently. It was in San Fernando that I had mahogany serving plates made for my family's Christmas present. We still use them. The most interesting trips, though, were those into the jungle surrounding the Post and continuing up the lower slopes of Mount Pinatuba, a volcanic cone just north. These trips

were especially fascinating because this small area was the home of a tribe of pygmies who lived in tiny grass shacks, hunted with bow and arrow and spear in the forest, and farmed little clearings. The only crop I saw was the *camote* (pronounced caw-mow-tee) which is a kind of sweet potato. These *Igorots* (ee-go-row-t), whom we called "Balugas," were friendly to their neighbors at Stotsenburg and were allowed on the base frequently. We saw (and smelled) them most often in the theater at the nightly movie, admission free. The women had a peculiar custom during these performances. They apparently loved the long, mild Filipino cigars, and would light up just before the show started. They smoked continuously, lighted end in the mouth, until the cigar was consumed. I never saw a woman get burned, nor did I see any remove ashes from their mouths. It didn't seem to hurt them, and though curious, I was never tempted to try it myself. Their speech was especially interesting: high-pitched, chirrupy voices like childrens', using a language that even the Filipinos did not understand. These people became a source of constant trouble later on to the occupying Japanese, who were hated by them. The Balugas used poisoned arrows on their enemies, caused many Japanese casualties and were very successful in avoiding the numerous attempts made to conquer them.

We had two houseboys, one assigned to each pair of us. The one I shared was named Jesus Cabatbat, a very young man of slight build. He was devoted, and did many things to make life easier and more pleasant. Through his good offices, we were able to acquire some cane furniture with cushions. He taught us to leave the lights burning in the closets to prevent mildew of leather goods in that humid climate, and to protect the gheko lizards which were ever present both indoors and out, because they kept the insect population to a manageable minimum. The longer he was with us, the more we appreciated his efforts, and we were very pleased for him when he announced his intention to marry. Of course we wanted to give him a suitable wedding present. When we asked what that might be, it was a shock to learn that he thought if we built him a house it would be nice. By stateside standards, this would be impossible, but the Islands were different. We found that a very adequate Nipa hut, which is what he had in mind, could be constructed for a mere two hundred and fifty *pesos*, or $125. Divided by four, this was not too expensive, so we had it built, to Jesus' undying gratitude. It was erected in his home barrio of *Sapangbato* (Sawpm-botto), near enough to the Post so that travel time did not interfere with either his duties or his new-found bliss. That investment was to be repaid, to me especially, many times over in so many ways.

Communication was always a problem for us on our forays into the surrounding countryside. There was no official language, even though the Philippines had been a US possession for forty-three years and formerly Spanish for several centuries. Most people spoke some Spanish and a few some English. The rest used one of approximately fifty native dialects, among them Tagalog and Pangasinan. It was so fragmented that in two adjacent barrios, the same words could have totally different meanings. For example, O-o (oh-oh) meant "yes" in Tagalog, but "no" in Pangasinan. Even so, the term *magundung dalaga* seemed universal. It means "pretty girl," and we all learned it very quickly. Since the War and the subsequent independence of the Philippine Republic, Tagalog has been adopted as the official language, though I suspect there are still many areas where it is not understood very well.

Speaking of *magundung dalaga,* there were none of them at Stotsenburg. About the end of October my new friend Art Derby and I obtained week-end leave to visit Manila and points south, to do some shopping and find some girls. We satisfied our yen for shopping very quickly when I bought a carved ivory chess set. But like all big cities, Manila could be cold and seemingly unfriendly to those without connections, and we didn't meet any willing *dalagas*. Consequently, we spent only one night and then went south to Pagsanjan, where there was a nice little hotel and other amenities centered around a spectacular waterfall in the middle of the jungle. The hotel was comfortable. There was a good small bar, and a restaurant that served poor quality meals, so we spent more time drinking than eating. During the day we swam in the pool below the falls and even took a banca trip down the rapids. The rest of the time, we sunned ourselves on the rocks and talked. Art was an unusual man. His parents had divorced many years before, and he had gone to live with his father in Mexico. They made their living by writing western stories for the pulp magazines at five cents a word. I asked him about the continuing need for new plots to keep readers interested. His reply was that they wrote by formula, keeping the same plot but changing the characters and order of events at will. As he described it, they didn't get rich but lived well. He was a very laid-back guy with a blonde crew-cut and a little potbelly, and was an interesting conversationalist. He did not survive the War, I'm sorry to say. After two relaxing days at Pagsanjan we went home, tanned, rested and ready to go to work again.

This trip marked the end of what had been a very pleasant interlude, but on our return to Stotsenburg we found that tensions had increased. As a result the entire post was on constant alert. This meant wearing sidearms at all times, and also intensified drilling and field exercises. Rumors abounded, most of them untrue but believed for a day or two nevertheless. Some of those rumors were wild, ranging in scope from the arrival of a brand new Naval fleet to the replacement of General Macarthur as the Commanding Officer of U.S. Forces in the Far East, with a great variety in between. Almost all were false but they gave us something to talk about. They also gave us the illusion that we were not quite so isolated from home as we thought.

One of the rumors which turned out a reality was that Manuel Quezon, then the President of the Philippines, was calling all the reserve Philippine Army to active duty.

The graduates of the military academy, located at Baguio in northern Luzon, would fill the major command positions and act as the training cadre. The balance of the officers and enlisted men would come from the reserve units. On paper, these reserve divisions existed and were being kept up-to-date on a continuing basis. They were supposed to be fully ready and equipped to take part in the defense of their country on short notice. We were to find the facts to be much different.

The mobilization order was issued early in November, 1941, and was preceded by the construction of training camps at several locations throughout the Islands. Typically, these consisted of nipa barracks, officers'quarters, headquarters buildings and storage areas, usually surrounding a parade ground. Nipa construction is minimal. The supporting structure is of bamboo or sawed lumber, tied or nailed together to form a framework. Floors, a foot or two above ground level, were split bamboo strips set far enough apart so that dirt and small debris would fall through. Walls extending up from the floor about four feet were woven from leaves or broadleaf grasses. From that point to the eaveline of the roof was open, except for hinged shutters which could be lowered to close during rainy weather. The roofs were thatch and there was no plumbing or electricity. It was easy to see why Jesus' house had cost so little.

About the same time the mobilization order was issued most of my class were promoted to First Lieutenant. Many, including me, also received new Orders detaching us from the Scouts and assigning us as Instructors to the newly activating Philippine Army.

4

The Philippine Army

My new assignment was to be an instructor to the Second Battalion of the Twenty-first Field Artillery (Philippine Army), which was just then in the process of mobilization. I was not particularly enthralled with that change because I had liked what I was doing and the people with whom I served. Some of the instructors were newly arrived from the States and others, like me, were transfers from the Scouts. Our regimental Chief Instructor was Col. Richard C. Mallonee. His Chief of Staff was Major Stanley B. Bonner, and also on Staff was 1st Lt. George Reed. The First Battalion Instructor was 1st Lt. Carl J. Savoie, and 1st Lt. Roderick K. Hendry had the responsibility for the Third Battalion. Though they had come to the Islands in one of the last ships, the Colonel and the Major had seen prior service in the Islands and were aware of some of the problems that would face us.

Col. Mallonee was originally from the Salt Lake City area and we developed a rapport partly based on that fact and partly on mutual respect. He was a veteran of World War I, during which he had commanded a battery of field artillery in France while a young Captain. He had a unique experience during that tour of duty. The commanding officer of any unit, when taking command, must sign for and become personally responsible for all the physical equipment assigned to his unit. Mallonee did this for his battery just before being shipped to France. His troops went on one ship and their guns and equipment on another but they never did meet on the other side. This required the issuance of new materiel before going into combat. For years after at about twelve-month intervals, Mallonee would receive a bill from the War Department for the lost equipment cost, about four hundred and ninety-six thousand dollars. Fortunately for him he was never forced to pay it, and apparently it had not affected his promotability. He was a very good professional officer.

Major Bonner, the only West Pointer in our group, was short and rotund. He had an acerbic wit which he used frequently to make a point, but he knew military practices thoroughly and we all liked him. His competence was of tremendous help during the subsequent months. I remember little of Lt. Reed, who did not stay with us for very long. Carl Savoie was a Cajun from Louisiana, a stocky strawberry blonde with a droll sense of humor, who liked people and became a favorite of the men in his battalion, as well as of his fellow instructors. Rod Hendry was much more reserved. He came from Grants Pass, Oregon, was short and of slight build with narrow features, and sported a black mustache. I believe he was the most competent of the junior instructors. In any case, we all enjoyed each other and worked well as a team. Our job was to supervise the training of the regiment and bring it up to combat readiness in the shortest possible time. If memory serves, The Philippine Army was composed of ten divisions. Each division had two infantry regiments, one artillery regiment and appropriate headquarters detachments. None of these had been activated prior to November of 1941. All of the enlisted men and almost all of the officers were reservists who, so far as I could tell, had received no previous training other than one or two meetings a year. It was a paper army in more ways than one. Little did we realize how short a time we had to accomplish our mission.

For our regiment, mobilization occurred early in November at a location not far from Stotsenburg. Inductees were supposed to arrive in uniform, but of the thousand men who made up the Twenty-first Field Artillery, most arrived bare-foot in blue cotton shorts and shirts with no collars. Some of them were wearing pith helmets made from pressed paper. Few had much personal equipment. With the exception of the Baguio graduates, it was difficult to distinguish between the officers and the soldiers, because not many had any insignia of rank or grade. Even fewer had a clear idea as to what was expected of them. However, we were finally able to sort out battery organizations and assemble the troops by unit. The next order of business was to issue clothing and equipment, and here the magnitude of our problem became really apparent. Only eight hundred blankets had been provided, and there were shoes (sneakers) for just over half the men. We had no steel helmets, side-arms or rifles. With respect to vehicles, major weapons and other items like communications equipment, the situation was much worse. For transport we had only one 4 x 4 command car and one Dodge 4 x 2 truck. There were a dozen field telephones, but no wire to connect them together. Fire control and survey instruments did not exist. The regiment had no ammunition, but that was all right because there weren't any guns either. Field kitchens and mess gear were missing. We were expected to shape this untrained mob into an army capable of fighting, but given no tools to do the job.

The regimental commander was Brigadier General Mateo Capinpin, and his second in command was Major Luis Villareal. These two, plus the three battalion commanders, constituted the only trained cadre. I don't remember the names of the other battalion leaders, but I worked directly with Captain Gregorio Mercado, commander of the Second Battalion, and we became quite friendly before the campaign was over. Even though he was a graduate of the military academy, he was a very young Captain, and nervous about holding a job ordinarily given to a Lieutenant Colonel. But he knew what had to be done and always did his best to see it was done correctly. Immediately after the equipment issue was completed, Gen. Capinpin issued an Officers' Call for all his officers and the instructor staff, and proceeded to lay out a program for the ensuing weeks based on the sorry conditions that prevailed. He also introduced us as Instructors and made it clear that, though we had no real authority under the tables of organization, and thus could not issue direct orders, any requests were to be obeyed as though they came from him personally. That edict was never rescinded and made our task much easier during the ensuing months. We became, in effect, de facto field commanders, a heady experience for young men only a few months out of college.

I admired the General. He was always concerned about his men, was aware of the problems they faced and was tireless in his attempts to solve the supply dilemma that faced us. In the absence of essential materiel, he and Col. Mallonee instituted a program of close-order drill, designed to get the troops acting as cohesive units and to get them used to the idea of executing orders without question. This continued every day except Sundays, and gradually evolved into open-order drill and infantry field tactics. In addition, we put together simulated field pieces (made from bamboo, of course) so that the gun crews could practice loading and firing sequences. Thus, things began to take shape and some semblance of order to emerge from the initial chaos. Almost all of the officers and men were young, and had come from the barrios and small towns in the province. For most, promotions had been political. They were unaccustomed to discipline and did not really understand the reasons for mobilization. Nonetheless, we made some progress in the first three weeks, enough so that Col. Mallonee, also a golfer, invited me to join him in a trip to Baguio for a game on the following Sunday—December 8, 1941.

In the interval, one of the lieutenants in the unit whose home was not far away, found that he was about to become a father. The mother-to-be was a local girl and they were not married. When this came to the General's attention he insisted on a wedding complete with *despedida*, a party corresponding to our reception. On this occasion, the affair took the form of an outdoor picnic. All the instructors were invited, and before the event, the Colonel established some ground rules. Most important of these was that we were guests in a foreign country, and depended for our success on the good will of our hosts. Therefore, we should be very careful not to offend by refusal of the food and drink offered. This sounded simple enough, but wasn't. First, the beer was warm and it also contained a Filipino delicacy—a *balut* (bah-loot). This little item is a dandy. It is a fertilized chicken egg about halfway along toward hatching which, after its shell is broken, is dropped into the warm beer. The drill is to chug-a-lug down the beer, with the final swallow containing the *balut*. It was a great temptation for me to ignore the Colonel's warning but I managed to get it down and, surprisingly, keep it down. Having passed this test, it didn't seem that anything else could faze me, but the main course turned out to be *lichon aso*, or stuffed dog. Its preparation involves selecting the animal, then starving it for a few days so that it is ravenous. At that point, a large container of cooked rice is given to the dog, which it eats with gusto, along with all the water it can hold. Its meal finished, the dog is killed immediately, skinned and prepared for roasting over an open fire. The appearance of this particular animal on the slowly rotating spit did nothing to improve my appetite. The poor creature had been scrawny to begin with, and without skin looked almost skeletal. Cooking odors were nowhere near the same as a beef roast, but were strong and somewhat rancid. After the bride and groom had been served, we, as honored guests, were given the choicest cuts. Mine was part of a hind quarter. By the end of the meal, it became my fervent hope that none of the other native officers would be forced into a similar marriage, and that I had attended my last *despedida*.

Back at the camp, training proceeded at an intensified rate with reasonably good results, so the Colonel and I felt optimistic about our projected trip to Baguio. We were to go there in his Buick. Sunday morning arrived and we loaded our clubs into the trunk, but before leaving, he wanted to listen to the news on the car radio and turned it on. After that old tube set warmed up, the first thing we heard was an announcement that changed our plans completely, for that day and forever. ''At ______ hours this morning, a day of infamy, the Japanese attacked Pearl Harbor with planes. Their bombing has inflicted heavy damage to ships and naval installations. . . .'' The broadcast went on to say that a state of war existed between our two countries and that all units presently in the Pacific were on full war alert. Although this happened December 7, 1941, for us it was December 8th, because we were on the other side of the International Date Line.

There we were with no guns, no transport, no field kitchens, nothing to fight with except the .45 caliber automatic pistols previously issued to the Instructors, and there was a war in progress. The reality of war was demonstrated to us forcefully later in the morning, when a flight of about twenty planes flew overhead, too high for us to distinguish their national insignia. At the same time, a lone fighter, clearly a P-40, climbed toward that formation, which then scattered, turned on it and shot it down. The plane crashed nearby and the pilot was still alive when we reached it. His only comment was, ''I thought they were ours.'' The Japanese aircraft continued south and with other flights, bombed Clark Field, Fort McKinley, Iba, the Naval base in Manila and other military targets. It was close to noon; all U.S. flights had been ordered to return to base and were positioned in neat rows on the flight line while the crews were fed. Most of our aircraft were destroyed by the fighters, called ''Zeros,'' and twin-engined bombers that in one series of raids eliminated nearly all American air power in the Philippines. Later, we learned that orders had been issued to ''let the Japanese strike the first blow,'' and refusing permission for the B-17 bombers to make strikes at Formosa or the Japanese naval forces. It was a stupid decision which cost us dearly; not surprising really, because war by its very nature is full of stupidities. We lost in those raids all but one or two of our B-17's and most of the fighters, in addition to naval ships and stores. These losses caused our own situation to become critical within a very short time, and seriously affected the ground forces' capability to defend the islands. The Japanese had gained the element of surprise with a vengeance.

5

To the Beach

Later that day, couriers began to arrive. They were necessary because we still had no usable telephones or radios. Some brought orders for deployment and promises for quick delivery of the many items we would need. Others performed readiness inspections. In long meetings, there were discussions of the situation, the plans to resolve it, and the possible help we could expect from the States. Nothing looked promising; indeed, our status was extremely grim. The havoc wreaked at Pearl Harbor and the resultant incapacity of the Navy to take any offensive action, coupled with the control the Japanese had in the air, both from their bases on Formosa (now Taiwan) and from aircraft carriers in the area, made it apparent that there was little hope for relief or resupply. We were truly on our own, and the assets we had on hand would have to do. There would be little more from any source, including Australia and Singapore, which would shortly be under siege themselves.

Our mission was to defend the Islands for as long as possible based on the assumption, later proved correct, that the Japanese would make a serious attempt to secure the entire western Pacific basin. Included would be China, where they had already been fighting for several years, Hong Kong, Singapore, Malaysia, Indo-China and finally Australia. The Philippines were a prime part of this plan, both as a target and as protection to Japan's flank as they made their progress to the south. All these places together were scheduled to become parts of the "Greater East Asia Co-Prosperity Sphere." Japan would be its chief beneficiary, gaining access to abundant raw materials, room to place excess population and markets for finished goods. The Japanese would at last feel free of the western influence that had rankled them ever since the Portugese traders first arrived in their country, about four centuries earlier.

Of the hundreds of islands that made up the Philippine chain, by far the most important was Luzon. It had the largest area, the only good deep-water port and most of the productive industrial capability. Other larger islands including Mindanao, Samar, Cebu, Panay, Negros and Mindoro, had no good ports and were largely agricultural; thus they were of small strategic importance. For these reasons, the plans for the defense of the Islands centered on Luzon, with only token military forces allocated to the others.

Potential landing sites on Luzon were limited. There was little of interest to the Japanese along the east coast of the island, primarily because there were few suitable beaches and no road network, making it very difficult to exploit any landing there. At the northern tip, Aparri offered better potential. It was close to their bases on Formosa and was connected to the central plain by two-lane paved highways in fair condition. Further south on the west coast were Vigan and San Fernando, with some of the advantages of Aparri, but the prime spot for a possible attack on the northern part of the island was considered to be Lingayen Gulf near the towns of Lingayen and

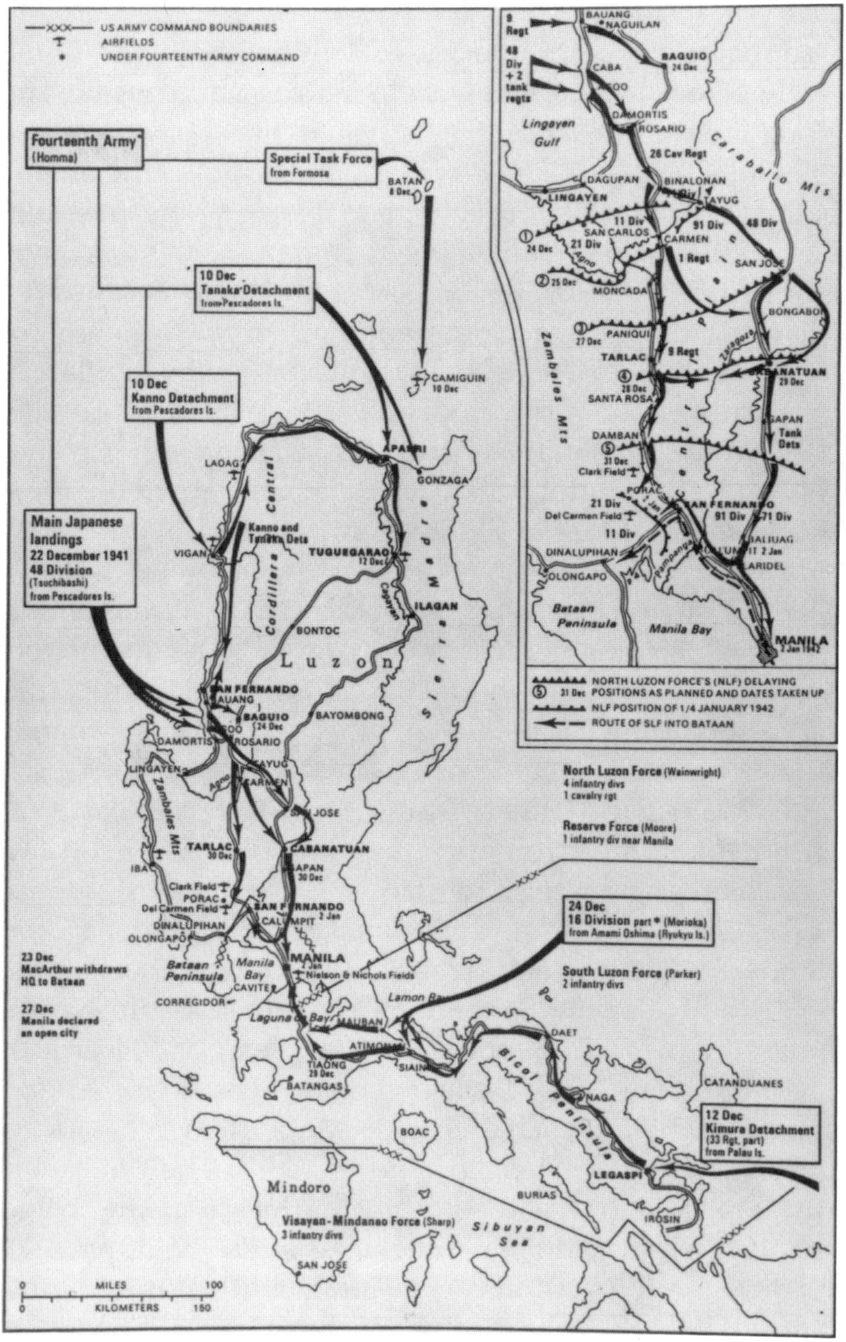

Japan Invades the Philippines: December 1941 - May 1942

Dagupan. This section had excelllent beaches and offered ready access to roads down the middle of the island and along the west coast. Subic Bay, a US naval base between the Gulf and Manila Bay, was not attractive to the enemy because of its isolation and poor development possibilities. Still further south, the next potential target was Manila Bay itself, thought to be impregnable because the island fortresses, Corregidor and Fort Drum, were guarding the entrance. The forts were buttressed by the Bataan Peninsula on the north side, and as long as these installations were functioning, Manila Bay was indeed safe. The last probable landing area was Legaspi, at the extreme southern tip of Luzon. It had easy access from the Pacific side, and there was a good road from there north to Manila. The master plan for defense took all these geographical factors into account. It proved to be remarkably accurate in its assumptions, because the Japanese did make successful assaults at all those places except Manila Bay.

The USAFFE (United States Armed Forces, Far East) was divided into two basic groups: the South Luzon Defense Force and the much larger North Luzon Defense Force, and two or three divisions based on Mindanao and Mindoro. General Parker was the commander in the South and General Johnathan Wainright in the North, under the over-all command of Gen. Douglas Macarthur. The Philippine Army Divisions were to have primary responsibility for beach defense. Mobile reserves, to be utilized where needed most, consisted of The Philippine Division, together with the 4th Marines and the 192nd and 194th Tank Battalions. Included in the Philippine Division were the 45th and 57th Infantry (PS), the 31st Infantry (US), the 26th Cavalry (PS) and the three Scout artillery battalions that had been based at Stotsenberg. So few airplanes were left that the Air Force became a negligible factor on the planning and was to be used primarily for reconnaisance and courier missions. The extra pilots and ground crews became infantry and were part of the mobile reserve, as a provisional infantry brigade.

Our 21st Division (PA) had the assignment of defending the beaches along the southern edge of Lingayen Gulf. My battalion was assigned to support the center, about midway between Lingayen and Dagupan, and was ordered to take up its position as soon as possible after the delivery of our guns and other equipment. This delivery began December 9th and continued through the 10th and 11th. It was not an occasion for much rejoicing. We were allocated antique materiel. Our weapons were British Model 1917, 75-millimeter guns with steel-tired wooden wheels. Ammunition consisted of high explosive shells with contact-detonating fuses and shrapnel rounds that had been stored in some warehouse as part of the excess from World War I. I hated that British gun because it was hard to maneuver, its range was not very great and it was inaccurate. In addition, the recoil cylinder was mounted over the gun barrel, making it difficult to bore-sight. The breech mechanism was low, and therefore was hard to operate. When you wanted to shoot the gun at its maximum elevation, it became a real knuckle-buster. The cannon had a single-piece tube trail with a spade at the end which limited the elevation of the barrel, and hence the range, that could be achieved. This weapon was nowhere near as good as the modified French 75 mm. guns we had used in the Scouts, and I missed them sorely.

The troops were issued small arms of similar vintage, turn-of-the-century Enfield bolt action rifles, somewhat like our own 30-06 Springfields but more difficult to operate. They were delivered in crates and were covered with Cosmoline, a rust preventing heavy grease almost impossible to remove without solvents, rags and lots of rubbing. The solvents were not included in the shipment. There were ancient field radios, telephones and other equipment as old and decrepit as the field guns and rifles.

Worse, there was no transport available and would not be for several days, which we did not have to spare. Savoie, Hendry and I were ordered to scout the surrounding area and commandeer anything on wheels that might prove useful. We managed to acquire about a dozen two-and-a-half ton civilian trucks with stake bodies, two pickups and three private automobiles. We signed chits on behalf of the Army which promised to pay their hesitant donors for the vehicles after the cessation of hostilities. These notes were honored; for over a year after the war I was verifying my signature to the War Department on them as they were presented for payment. One of the cars, which I appropriated for my own use, was an early model Ford V-8 two door sedan. Its owner was an Irish Catholic priest, reluctant but philosophical about parting with his chariot, because he knew he would lose it anyway sooner or later. To help ease his pain I gave him my last bottle of Scotch.

As soon as we had gathered the trucks together, we began to move our regiment to the beach. It took several trips for two days to get the job done. First out were the guns, because they had to be loaded up on top, rather than the normal procedure of being towed. Towing was impractical because the wooden wheels would have come apart if moved at more than a crawl over paved highway. They had been designed as slow-moving horse-drawn equipment and there were no shock absorbing devices installed.

Next came ammunition and the communications equipment, and finally all the miscellaneous items and personal gear. Non-essentials were shipped to storage at Stotsenburg, and that was the last I ever saw of my golf clubs and typewriter. The entire move would have taken longer had we not found the Filipinos were unaware of the meaning of the word ''overload.'' It was their idea that a truck was full only when things began to fall off the top.

During all this confusion we continued to train the gun crews at an intensive pace born of desperation. Somehow we had to mold this unit of barefoot boys into a fighting force in a few days or weeks, not the months that had been anticipated. Gun drills, siting, loading and firing practice went on every day, mingled with the additional training necessary for a soldier. This included infantry tactics, military courtesy, first aid, sanitation, the use of survey and fire-control equipment, and the functions of the observation post. We taught the officers first, then assisted them in teaching enlisted men. Some concepts were very difficult to convey. For example, a gun must be put in position and backed into a ''trail log,'' which holds it securely in place and absorbs part of the recoil when it is fired. It seemed impossible to get this across. We could not demonstrate because we were under orders not to fire the guns until an actual landing attempt occurred. Our neophytes asked why they couldn't just bury the trail spade deep in the sand. There was no good way to answer this until finally, the General granted permission to fire a very few rounds to demonstrate, both with and without the trail log. It was a convincing show. The unrestrained gun would buck and jump and scoot backward in random directions, then had to be worked into position again and carefully re-sited. Though exciting, it was extremely dangerous to the gun crew and made accurate shooting virtually impossible. As a result of the demonstration, the men felled palm trees everywhere, which furnished good trail logs but ruined what little camouflage there had been.

Sanitation and personal protection also concerned us very much. "Why dig a slit trench (field toilet) when there is the ocean right in front of us, and the tides clean up the beach every day?" Barrio life had not prepared our men to cope with the problems generated by large numbers of people confined to a relatively small area. None had ever been under fire and so did not realize how much shelter a foxhole could provide against bullets and shrapnel. This of course, we could not demonstrate, and it was a constant frustration throughout the campaign to see that foxholes were dug and maintained. I do not cite these examples in complaint. The men were eager and motivated to learn, especially now that hostilities had commenced and they were defending their homeland. It was simply that there was a whole living system to change in a hurry, and for those unsophisticated people that was very difficult. But we persisted and they did learn. The Filipinos' very eagerness constituted a hazard. If we issued an order, personal follow-up was necessary to ensure its completion, because if you only asked about its progress, you would often get untrue verbal assurances. To please an officer was important to them, so most would tell what they knew he wanted to hear, rather than the more unpleasant truth.

Life in the field was was primitive. Everyone slept on the ground wrapped in his blanket or bedroll and there were no tents. Small groups cooked their simple meals together over open fires, located behind the trees away from the beach for maximum concealment. The diet consisted mostly of rice and beans, with occasional meat issues and fruit garnered from the countryside. Mosquitoes are always a problem in the tropics and we had little protection against them. Very few possessed mosquito bars, a cheesecloth canopy hung over the bed, which is supposed to keep out the insects. This was one reason that as the war progressed, more and more people, Filipinos and Americans alike, were afflicted with the malaria that became almost as much of a killer as the bullets. I was one of the lucky ones who escaped it. We were able to rotate a few men at a time into the adjacent towns for a few hours so that they could visit with family and friends and relax a little from the constant training grind. Otherwise it was a dull existence: work, eat, sleep, wash and repair clothing.

My own life was not too bad. The instructors had their own mess, so the food was alright. We all had cots and bedrolls and were comfortable. Jesus Cabatbat showed up after we had been at the beach for a week or so, wanting to enlist and to become my orderly. This was permitted, and he stayed with me to the end, becoming a friend as well as taking care of all my personal needs. My bedroll was always prepared and clean, my uniforms the same, though not to the standards we knew at Stotsenburg. The simple food we had was served with a flourish, in spite of the fact that the utensils used were only GI aluminum mess-kits. Jesus was a message runner and a second set of eyes, providing extra protection for me under combat conditions. He even had time to teach me to speak a little Tagalog and help me to understand some of the problems his people were facing in their forced and sudden jump into the twentieth century.

6

Waiting

It is nearly impossible to keep motivation at a high pitch when nothing out of the ordinary is happening. Although we, as instructors, were grateful for the time given us to train our units, the men became restless and a little bored with inactivity interrupted only by constant drilling in their duties. Given our state of preparedness at the time of Pearl Harbor and the air attacks on our airfields and other installations, the Japanese could have conquered the Philippines much earlier and with few losses if they had started their invasion immediately thereafter. But they didn't, probably because they may not have expected to score such an outstanding success in those early weeks, and consequently were not prepared to exploit that advantage to its fullest. Also, it takes much time and organization to mount even a small landing force, and they were already over-extended in their Pacific operations. As it was, they allowed us to prepare partially, and ultimately, that cost them dearly.

Whatever the reason, we gained that small advantage, and used the extra time to good purpose. We had heard that some of the warehouses at Fort Stotsenburg were undamaged, or only slightly so, and that they contained foodstuffs, clothing and other items that could be very useful to us. I took a couple of our new trucks down, along with a small crew of men, to see what could be had. Considering our supply situation, what we got was a bonanza. We were able to fill out most of the clothing shortages that had so plagued us and also to obtain many other useful items. In addition, after making two trips, we had a stock of rice and canned goods that formed an essential supplement to the meager rations furnished through official channels. It was enough to keep ourselves and our troops in fairly good condition until we finally backed up into Bataan in January. We were also able to save a stock of reasonably good liquor (under those circumstances, all liquor is good) from being captured by the enemy, and we consumed it happily until the last bottle ran dry a few weeks later. Moderation was not a factor and that whiskey became an effective palliative for battlefield boredom. I imbibed my share of the liquid therapy at the end of each long frustrating day.

Our major problem was still transportation, primarily of those outmoded guns. We had heard that the Army was to be supplied with a new type of self-propelled artillery, though we had only a vague idea what it might look like. However, that did give us an idea—why not make our own? It would solve the problem of the wooden wheels if successful, and greatly accelerate our movement when that became necessary. The American instructors had a brainstorming session wherein we laid out a tentative design involving the commandeered civilian trucks. It provided for a beefed-up flat bed on the truck, a built-up trail log to absorb shock and simplify gun-laying, some means of preventing the gun from jumping over the side during transportation and firing, and a working storage for ammunition, if feasible. I was deputed to scout the area and find some facility that could do the conversion. I took Mercado along with me as interpreter/adviser. The first place we went was Dagupan, where we found exactly what we needed. Resident there was Mark Thomas, an expatriate American married to a Filipina, who operated a garage and car repair business. In addition, he was in charge of maintenance for the northern division of Pangasinan Transportation Company (Pantranco). He had retired from the Service years before and elected to remain in the pleasant ambience of the Islands. When first approached he was skeptical. He said, ''You guys must be nuts! That thing will be so high you couldn't hide it behind a three-story building.'' But he finally became intrigued by our plan and eager to try its implementation. Thomas contributed many good ideas to its ultimate completion as we worked through the problem.

A major concern was obtaining sufficient materials, which we knew would be difficult in Dagupan. I have referred to it as a city but it really was not, being instead more analogous to the small towns that dot the rural areas of our own country. The highway was the only paved street; the rest were dusty paths laid out in a roughly rectangular pattern. There were no sidewalks other than an occasional duck-board here and there. The shops facing the main street were the usual mix of restaurants, bars and small retail stores, a hardware store and a few service businesses which catered to the farms in the area. The homes were mostly the ubiquitous nipa hut, one- or two-room structures built high on stilts. The more substantial houses followed the same general pattern, though they were larger and better built. The ground level area of all was used as garage, for storage or for livestock: pigs, chickens, even a carabao. Living quarters for the family were six or seven feet above that, in order to obtain the maximum benefit of the ocean breezes. The better houses had indoor plumbing, but most depended for water on wells or a tap located centrally among the huts, and used a hole in the floor for waste disposal. Water heaters were unknown and un-needed in that warm climate. The people were friendly but a little wary of gringos. Supplies of everything but the basics were very limited, and we had to make many substitutions before we finished our task.

The resulting Philippine Army version of self-propelled artillery was ugly, but it worked. First, we in-

Self-propelled field artillery, home made

stalled a set of heavy-duty shock-absorbers and extra leaves in the springs. Next, we strengthened the bed by adding a layer of three-inch hardwood planks on top of the original ones. Then, behind the cab and facing the rear, we constructed a storage rack big enough to contain seventy-two slots for ammunition, four layers high and eighteen wide. We positioned the gun, pointing to the rear, so that its axle position, and center of gravity, was directly over the rear axle of the truck. In turn, this determined the position of the trail spade. There we built a trail log, using another two layers of three-inch plank shaped into an arc. This would allow the gun to be turned approximately ten degrees to the right or left about its vertical axis and still remain in contact with something solid. All the flooring and the trail log were bolted into place for strength and stability. We still had a problem: when a light artillery piece is fired, the vertical component of the recoil force makes it jump. To minimize this, and to keep the weapon from jumping off the truck, we had to devise some sort of restraint. It was accomplished by embedding a heavy eye-bolt in our platform on each side, directly over the truck wheels and directly under the hub of the gun axle, which had a steel ring attached to it. Half-inch strips were cut from the tapered liners usually placed between the truck wheel and the tube inside the tire, and then woven into rubber ropes. With the gun on the truck bed, the tensioned rubber ropes were looped through the eye-bolt and the ring several times, and securely fastened with U-bolt clamps. This formed a primitive spring-like tie-down, and we hoped it would keep the gun securely in place. Last, we installed a removable pin through the lunette ring into a hole drilled in the trail log, that would keep the gun pointing straight to the rear while traveling. We found there was ample room for the gun crew to function with everything in place.

Finally, in a surprisingly short time, the first unit was ready and we drove it back to the camp for inspection by the Colonel and the General. It appeared ungainly, standing so high in the air that effective camouflage would be difficult (it could be hidden behind a two-story building), but it was maneuverable. Testing was to be simple and certainly could not follow the procedures of an Army Proving Ground, but would consist only of firing a few rounds from the gun. If the contraption held together and did not kill the crew, we had a useful weapon. That was the way we tested it, and it worked like a charm. We backed the unit up close to the beach and shifted gears into neutral, chocked the wheels but didn't set the brakes, loaded and fired. Everything hung together, the gun stayed on the truck-bed and the recoil did no damage. Voila! General Capinpin was delighted and Col. Mallonee grinned like a Cheshire cat. They gave me orders to make as many more as time and materials would allow before the Japanese tried to begin their invasion in our sector.

Those orders were welcome to me for a number of reasons. A major one was that our American garage-owner had two lovely mestiza daughters, about nineteen years old, who managed to be in or near the building any time I was. They were interested and so was I and I would have fallen in love, but couldn't choose between them. Later, I wished I had been just as deliberate in July about the decision to go to the Philippines in the first place. Though I tried, I was never able to find out what had happened to them after the enemy occupied Dagupan. The Thomases were good people and had been nice to me during a trying time, giving me freedom in their home and a warm welcome at their table.

Our garage-cum-arsenal was running out of supplies, so I had to scout all through the area for materials, and developed quite a reputation as a forager in the process. ''Foraging'' is a euphemism for scrounging. We managed to collect enough wood, metal and fittings to complete the second conversion. This one went faster because there was not so much cut-and-fit involved and by now we knew exactly what we wanted. The second one also worked well during the tests, so we ended up with a full platoon of self-propelled artillery. I was proud of that platoon and felt a keen sense of personal accomplishment at my first creative endeavor. Competition for places on the crews that were to serve these guns was vigorous, and we were able to select the best men from the battalion. The platoon was regarded as an elite unit, especially since those who were selected got immediate promotions, so that there was nothing less than a PFC in it. Privates were immediately promoted to at least PFC: all were advanced one grade in rank. Esprit was high and that platoon worked very hard.

In the meantime, tension was building. Our reconnaisance patrols had reported a concentration of ships northward from Luzon, and we knew that a landing attempt was imminent, though we did not yet know the intended target. Everyone was jumpy, even those who had been bored and discontented with the relative inactivity of the past few weeks. We assigned guard duty twenty-four hours a day, with at least a third of our men awake at any given time, and it resulted in our only real exciting incident. One night about eleven o'clock, an observer thought he saw ships in the Gulf. He immediately reported this to his superior who, without waiting to check, ordered a barrage on the supposed location of the invasion fleet. Since he had not bothered to specify either high-explosive ammunition or shrapnel, they fired whatever came to hand. It was the middle of the night and I was asleep. The opening shot, followed by many others in close succession, brought me to my feet and I ran to the beach, shirt-tails flapping and shoelaces dragging in the sand. I found all the gun crews busy and excited because they thought they were finally confronting the enemy. When we determined the facts, we found there was nothing in the gulf that even remotely resembled an invasion fleet, and a cease-fire was ordered. After the commotion died down and trigger-fingers were relaxed, it turned out that the first few rounds our guns fired had been shrapnel, which exploded above the water surface of the gulf. Thinking that these explosions were a return attack from the enemy, the battery officers ordered an increase in their rate of fire, causing still more airbursts and compounding the problem still further. Thus, we expended a considerable amount of ammunition to no purpose.

When I discussed this with Greg Mercado, he shrugged it off with the statement that they were probably firing at *aswans,* which means ghosts. Whatever the answer, it went on to serve as an example of what a press corps, hungry for news it can print, will do. The next morning's broadcast was full of word that the Japanese had been repulsed at Lingayen with heavy losses in their first attempt to invade. This was picked up by the news services and transmitted to the States as a major accomplishment for the USAFFE. So far as I know, none of these false statements were ever retracted or corrected, and the detailed histories of the defense of the Philippines probably still carry it as a claimed victory. For those of us who were there, it was an embarrassment. For me personally, this alarm proved that I could function under pressure reasonably well, even though I was scared to death at first.

Finally, however, there was a landing, at Aparri. The defenses against it collapsed in short order and the Japanese began to move south. Part of the reserve committed to halt this advance was the 26th Cavalry, which fought brilliantly before being forced to retreat. Incidentally, to my knowledge at least, the Philippine campaign was the last where mounted cavalry were utilized in modern warfare. From that period, horses were replaced by tanks, and the cavalry became identified as ''Armor.'' These troops were great in that mountainous terrain and were able to delay the southward advance of the enemy for several days as support for the Philippine Army 41st Division in that sector. In an attempt to flank these defensive forces, the Japanese also tried a landing at Vigan. It too was successful, and forced our troops to withdraw still further to the vicinity of San Fernando, La Union. By now, the Twenty-first Division was fully convinced that it was next, and we could expect that we would see our own real confrontation very shortly.

It didn't happen quite that way, however. There was a landing at Legaspi in the south coincident with the one at Aparri. this one also was successful and since the forces opposing it were small, was developed immediately. It became necessary for Gen. Parker to begin the withdrawal of his South Luzon Corps northward toward Manila very soon after the landing. The master plan called for the simultaneous retreat of both the northern and the southern USAFFE forces into the Bataan peninsula for the final defense of the Island. It became clear that the Southern Defense Force would not be able to impede the Japanese advance significantly, and they began their withdrawal to, and through, Manila in short order. They had to move north fast, because the Japanese had also landed at Lamon Bay, not far south of Manila on the east coast, and could have cut Parker off with ease. Headquarters had decided that Manila could not be defended adequately in this fluid situation against a well-organized enemy. It was therefore declared an ''open city'' in the hope that it could be spared damage in its occupation by pointless fighting in the streets. It was a vain hope; Japan's bombers hit Manila anyway, causing many civilian casualties and a lot of physical damage to no purpose.

These events demanded that the North Luzon Force begin its own retreat into Bataan before the bulk of its units had been engaged, in order to avoid being cut off in our rear by the Japanese advancing from the south. We left the beach, somewhat disappointed that there had been no chance for action, but recognizing that if we didn't go then, there wouldn't be much opportunity later. The only bright spot in all this was that, just before the abandonment of our defense area, we finally received some additional trucks, 4 x 4's equipped for towing as well as carrying. There were eight of them for our battalion, and we elected to use six for towing the remainder of our guns even though that would cause such damage to their wheels. Our self-propelled units could take care of themselves. The new vehicles did make it possible to move all our equipment and most of the personnel at one time without requiring a second trip. Some men would have to walk, but that was normal procedure.

7

Retreat to Bataan

There were paved highways leading south from the Lingayen Gulf toward Manila: Highway 3 down the center of the island, another along the Zambales coast bordering the China Sea and a third, Highway 5, through the Cagayen Valley in the eastern half of the island. The coastal road was essentially denied to us, because long portions of it were highly visible to the increasing numbers of Japanese patrol vessels operating in the China Sea. Harassing fire from them could have halted the movement of military convoys with ease. This left Highways Three and Five as the only practical routes to use, barring occasional dirt roads and trails not capable of handling any great volume of vehicular traffic. From the Lingayen sector, Highway Three was our only choice. In scouting for alternate routes, we did discover that construction had started on a new highway parallel to it. Watching this project was like looking through a window into the past. It could not possibly have been completed in the time we had available, with the methods being used to build it. For earthmoving they were using Fresno scrapers, a hand-dump type pulled by slow-moving carabao, which had not been used in the States since the early twenties. The workers were also carrying dirt in baskets suspended from a wooden neck yoke. Although the process was interesting for me to watch, it had nothing to do with our immediate problem because the new road started and ended nowhere.

We had to move large numbers of men and much equipment to the rear, under pressure from the enemy behind us, without having our retreat become a rout. It was accomplished with great difficulty because the road was choked with vehicles and marching troops, mixed together, seemingly without route plan or fixed destination. The roar of motors assaulted the ears and a constant pall of thick dust hung in the air, fraying the nerves and making tempers short, including mine. The fear of bombing and strafing by the Japanese air force, like that at Clark Field, Iba, Nichols Field and the Port Area of Manila, gnawed at our vitals constantly. For reasons known only to themselves the enemy failed to grasp this opportunity and allowed the movement to take place without incident. At this point I began to know the acid taste of fear and helplessness well, and it never entirely left me for the rest of the campaign. We could have been excellent targets because we had to stay on the roads in the open. There were long lines of men moving at route step, interspersed with trucks and artillery, all creeping at a snail's pace. Even though I had my little Ford, I could not move up and down the column to help when the inevitable traffic jams occurred, because two-way movement was not possible on that crowded, narrow road. I found a place near the center of our battalion and was forced to hold it regardless of what happened around me. All of us drove with our heads out the window trying to spot enemy aircraft in time to scatter into the bushes before the strafing began. That it didn't happen, did nothing to relieve our tension.

The master defense plan included execution of delaying actions at several pre-selected positions; the first was on the Agno River about ten miles south of Dagupan. We reached it and set up the defense line, but occupied it only for a day or two. The Japanese reinforced their invasion troops from ships at Lingayen and were using tanks to good advantage against the divisions on our right flank. Our own left flank suffered a strong attack and both flanks were forced back. The center position became untenable so, without firing a shot, we pulled out. The movement was a repetition of the first days march, just as much dust and noise and confusion, but with the additional strain of knowing that our enemy was close behind and pressing hard. Our next line stretched from Cabanatuan on the east through Tarlac in the center and on to the mountains in the west. The Twenty-first Division was stationed at Tarlac. This defense position was supposed to have been already prepared, with gun emplacements dug and supplies provided. Nothing was there, but in spite of that we had emplaced the guns, sighted them in and fired ranging rounds before nightfall. Time had ceased to have much meaning in the hurly-burly of these activities, so I can't remember the date, except that it was near Christmas.

Here the division had its first battle experience. Our forward observers reported enemy activity in front of our sector early the next morning, and they launched an attack on the infantry soon after. We were called upon for supporting fire, this time not at *aswans*. We must have inflicted some damage, because the pressure on the front line eased for a while. Fire control was visually directed by the observation post, where I spent about half of my time. Usually, the observation post is a necessary forward adjunct to precise maps prepared by Army cartographers, and used in the fire direction center for control of artillery fire and target selection, but we never did have that luxury. The best and only chart we had was a road map issued by the Standard Oil Company, not good for precision work but better than nothing, so we depended almost entirely on the observation post. In spite of that deficiency, we were able to provide good support to the infantry and disrupt the Japanese plans for a while.

Savoie's battalion distinguished itself by holding off a Japanese column at one of the bridges for several hours, finally destroying the bridge before retiring. The normal order of battle is that the front line is held by the infantry, supported by field artillery placed a thousand yards or so behind. This day, Savoie found that the troops in front of him had disappeared and his guns were now facing the Japanese directly. Using such cumbersome weapons, this is unhealthy as hell, and he should logically have moved out immediately, but did not. Through the force of his strong personality and personal example, he was able to rally his own men and complete their mission. Only then did they move back behind the infantry cover. He was recommended for a Silver Star because of that action, and deserved it.

This engagement was the first time our battalions had come under fire from enemy artillery. From the observation post (OP) we had no trouble spotting the muzzle blasts of their guns. The incoming shells whined toward us, the sound culminating in an explosion when they hit the ground. Shell fragments made the noise of a swarm of angry bees as they buzzed through the trees and underbrush. We had a few casualties, some slight wounds from those jagged bits of metal, but little real damage was sustained by personnel or equipment. I was proud of our men, who had so recently been only simple farmers, but were developing into pretty good soldiers under very adverse circumstances and were doing well in combat conditions. I would never have said so to anyone but I was a little proud of my own reactions, too. Although I never became blase about being shelled, it was not the fearsome thing I had envisioned. The bombardment had one good side effect. At last our men were convinced that fox-holes had some value and we never after had much trouble in getting them dug. As a matter of fact, some were dug too deep, and caved in as a result.

In addition to the ground fighting, we also had our first aerial attacks while at Tarlac. Our guns were under cover, but muzzle blasts gave their positions away to the small observation plane circling overhead. We called him "Charley" and developed a sincere hatred for him, especially since there was nothing we could do to stop his activity. Our truck park and command post were to the rear of the guns and well dispersed under the trees. They were out of sight from the air, but there had been no opportunity to obliterate the tracks leading in, so Charley had no trouble locating them. Mid-morning brought the first bombing raids by the twin-engine aircraft we learned to identify as "Betsy's," which dropped hundred pound bombs on our installation, from about five thousand feet, for the rest of the morning. There wasn't a great deal of damage except to the nerves, but the din of explosions all around and the huge clouds of dust raised by them caused much irrational activity and some panic in all of us. As time passed, these raids became fairly routine, sometimes occurring by themselves and sometimes accompanied by strafing from the Zeros that formed their

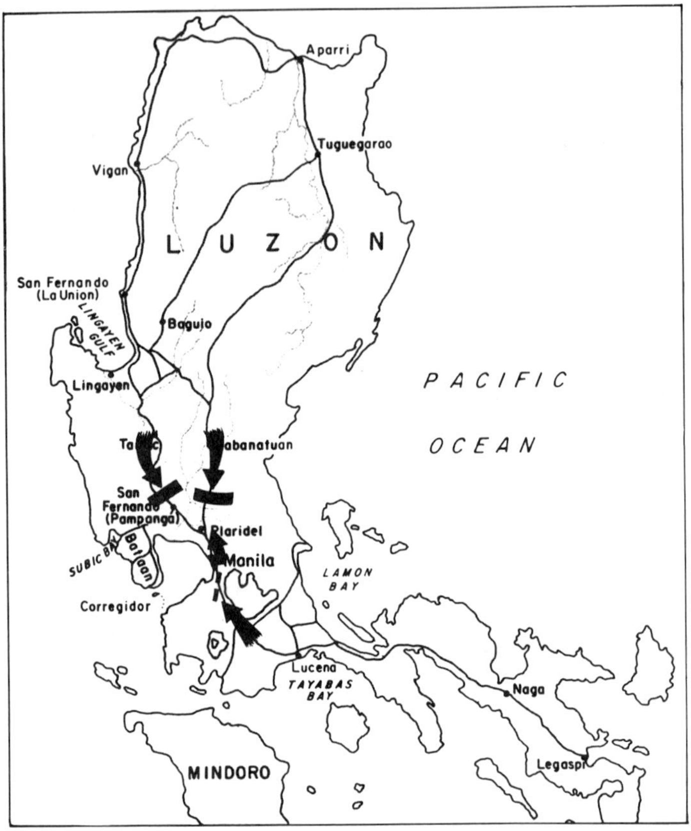

MacArthur's Problem:
Withdrawal through Defile into Bataan, December 1941

fighter escort. We learned to spot the bomb release point and could determine from that whether we were in the bulls-eye or not. If not, we went about our business more or less as usual. However, this technique was not infallible, and there were enough unpleasant surprises to keep us on edge any time the sound of airplane engines could be heard.

While all this was going on, the situation to the east and south was deteriorating rapidly. The South Luzon Force was being pushed back steadily. Homma (the Japanese commanding general) was exerting heavy pressure on our right flank south of Cabanatuan, and it was beginning to fold. In their retreat, both forces had to use the roads almost exclusively. In order to approach Bataan, they needed to reach the junction with Highway Three at Plaridel, then turn northward to San Fernando, Pampanga, to get on the road into the peninsula. In between Plaridel and San Fernando was the Pampanga River, which the highway crossed via the Calumpit Bridge. It was vital to protect that bridge until the last of the retreating troops had cleared. The entire movement was complicated because in additon to the troops, there were many civilians fleeing Manila to the perceived protection of Bataan, using the same road net. All told, at least ninety thousand people would have to cross the Calumpit Bridge before the Japanese arrived.

We were ordered to abandon the Tarlac position and shorten our lines by moving back to the vicinity of Bambam. Our new line extended from Mount Arayat on the west, through Bambam and terminated in the Pampanga River marshes on the east flank. It was to become the last defense we would make prior to our own entry into Bataan, and we had to hold the position until all those thousands had reached and cleared San Fernando behind us. The move would be more difficult than the one into Tarlac. It had to be over a two-lane road with narrow shoulders ending in steep banks down to the countryside level. Rice paddies bordered the road, so expanding the route was impossible.

This transit was most trying. Trucks, guns and personnel all crowded into one channel with no means of clearing the way. If a vehicle stalled and could not be restarted, it was merely pushed over the side and abandoned. Not much time was wasted in futile attempts to save the loads. The noise was deafening, the usual dust hung heavy in the air, and the division personnel, now fearful and disoriented, were almost impossible to control. In the midst of all this confusion, an American general drove up from the south in a command car, halted the column and ordered it to turn around and re-ocupy the positions we had just left. I suspected that he was drunk at the time, and later on this was proved correct. Certainly he did not understand, perhaps did not know, the predicament faced by those retreating to Bataan. Whatever his thinking, it cost our column several hours and the loss of much equipment, several trucks and more important, a significant part of our food supplies. Ultimately, those losses would cause the deaths of several hundred men, women and children. This man is long since dead, but there were many of us present that day who would cheerfully have killed the son-of-a-bitch on the spot. Even today, more than forty-seven years later, I can see him standing in the back of a command car waving his arms and shouting at his subordinates. That memory is still fresh in my mind, and never fails to renew the anger and despair his interference caused.

We finally reached our assigned area near Bambam and, by the time our guns were emplaced, were exhausted, angry at the whole world and dispirited. We had had nothing to eat in over twenty-four hours and hunger gnawed at us the same way it had for that poor dog at the *despedida*. Again, the only saving grace in the whole episode was that the Japanese failed to harass the moving column from the air. In fact, they did very little of this to any of the retreating Luzon Forces, for reasons that are still inexplicable to me, but for which I will be eternally grateful. I remember this day vividly for its confusion, frustration and misery. It was New Year's Eve.

The next day was January 1, 1942. We moved again, a short distance south of San Fernando to Guagua, together with another Philippine Army division. We were expected to hold this position long enough for the last of the other forces to make their final move into Bataan. They cleared the Calumpit Bridge that afternoon and it was destroyed behind them. We held our post for two or three days without much pressure from the enemy. They must have been too busy consolidating their gains and regrouping to follow up very vigorously. Finally, all the defenders, including ourselves, were confined in that small peninsula, about twenty miles wide at the base and twenty-five miles long to the tip. The Japanese now occupied all of Luzon, with the exception of Bataan and Corregidor and a couple of small island forts just south of Corregidor. There were over a hundred thousand persons, both civilian and military, trapped in Bataan. The entire garrison was exhausted. We had lost much of our already inadequate supply of weapons and amunition, and there was not enough food to take care of half our number for more than eighty or ninety days.

I would be remiss if I ignored the contributions of the Philippine Division and related units, including the 45th and 57th Infantry, the artillery battalions and the 26th Cavalry. Together with the 192nd and 194th Tank battalions, the 31st Infantry and the 4th Marines, they performed the herculean task of protecting our flanks and delaying the enemy's advance at many points along the path of retreat. They lost much of their strength in both personnel and equipment along the way, and their efforts earned the undying gratitude of all of us. In the beginning, I had thought that the Philippine Division would have been better utilized as cadres for the training of the Philippine Army, which shows how wrong I was. If it hadn't been for that Division and the other units bridging the gaps left here and there by panic-stricken infantry fleeing the front lines, the whole defense effort could have collapsed very early, freeing the Japanese from a costly campaign and opening for them the way to Australia.

8

The Battle for Bataan

After the North and South Luzon Forces withdrew into the Bataan Peninsula in the early part of January, 1942, it took the Japanese slightly over three months to effect a final victory over us. The story of that victory is one of bloodshed and hardship, heroism and cowardice, hunger and deprivation. To understand it requires some knowledge of the terrain and the conditions under which we fought.

The peninsula is the southern extension of the mountain range that borders the western coast of Luzon from Lingayen Gulf on the north to Mariveles at its southern tip. There are three major peaks in this range that are situated within Bataan. The northernmost is Mt. Natib (nah-teeb), in the center is Mt. Samat (saw-mawt) and the most southerly is Mt. Bataan. From the ridge line formed by these three the land slopes gently east toward Manila Bay. The western slope is much steeper, plunging into the China Sea sharply and having few beaches suitable for an enemy to use for landing. Bataan was lightly populated at that time. There were small agricultural towns, with a few hundred inhabitants each, along the periphery, but none in the interior. At the northern extreme on the west coast was Olongapo and the naval base at Subic Bay. The first town south of Olongapo was Moron, ten miles or so away, and south of Moron was Bagac, with Mariveles at the tip of the peninsula. There were more on the bay side of Bataan. They were, in order from south to north, Cabcaben, Lamao, Limay, Orion, Pilar, Balanga, Abucay, Lubao, Orani and Dinalupihan. The road net was primitive and consisted of a narrow dirt track from Moron to Mariveles, which joined with the lightly paved two-lane road from Marivales through Dinalupihan, meeting Highway 3 at San Fernando. The only cross-peninsular connection was a narrow unpaved road, not much more than a trail, between Pilar and Bagac. We also depended on footpaths, made by hunters, through the jungle that overlaid the entire area. About two or three miles south across the bay from Mariveles was the island fortress of Corregidor, and not far south of there was Fort Drum, so small that it was called it ''the concrete battleship.'' The Navy base at Subic Bay was abandoned very early because its isolation made it indefensible. Mariveles, due to its close proximity to Corregidor, was transformed into a second-rate military and naval base. We didn't need much more because our remaining navy was very small, consisting of a few gunboats and a submarine tender.

The strategic plans for the defense of Manila Bay had been based on two assumptions: first, that any attack would come from ships via the China Sea, and second, that the Bataan forces could protect Corregidor long enough to allow for the arrival of a relief fleet. These very old plans were made before aircraft were used to any great extent, and therefore did not allow for the large-scale use of fighters and bombers. Also, the debacle at Pearl Harbor grossly reduced the capacity of our Navy to provide protection from the air. In an attempt to provide such protection, a battalion of mobile anti-aircraft artillery had been installed, but there were too few weapons in that battalion to be a really effective deterrent. Furthermore, Corregidor's big guns were pointed seaward to guard against attacking ships, and could not be traversed far enough to the right to be brought to bear on Bataan if that became necessary; only a few 12-inch mortars had that capability. For these reasons, the survival of Bataan was essential to the protection of Corregidor and to the denial of access to Manila Bay by the enemy. It was a case of doing the best we could with the men and materiel at hand.

While the retreat into Bataan was in progress, Manila had been evacuated by Macarthur and the USAFFE headquarters, who were transferred by boat to Corregidor. New headquarters were set up in Malinta Tunnel and the lateral tunnels extending from it. This move earned for Macarthur the sobriquet, "Dugout Doug," pinned on him by troops fighting in the mountainous jungles of Bataan. How he must have hated that name! Subordinate headquarters were established in Bataan. One of the first tasks of the latter was to determine how well we would be able to perform our defense mission, and the results of the study were most discouraging. There was equipment for two field hospitals, left-over from World War I, outdated and partly useless because of inevitable deterioration during the intervening decades. They had limited medication, anaesthetic and surgical supplies, and little tentage for the protection of patients or hospital staff. Some of the nurses had to sleep in old Pambusco busses without windows. It was found that there was ammunition for most of the old weapons we had. Gasoline for the vehicles was in short supply, and spare parts were non-existent. But the major problem, then and later, was that there was food for much less than half of the hundred-odd thousand people in Bataan. The planners seemed to have been more interested in providing the materiel necessary for fighting than they were for the physical well-being of those who fought. To add to that oversight, none of them had considered that, in addition to the soldiers, there would be refugees who had to be fed and cared for, twenty-six

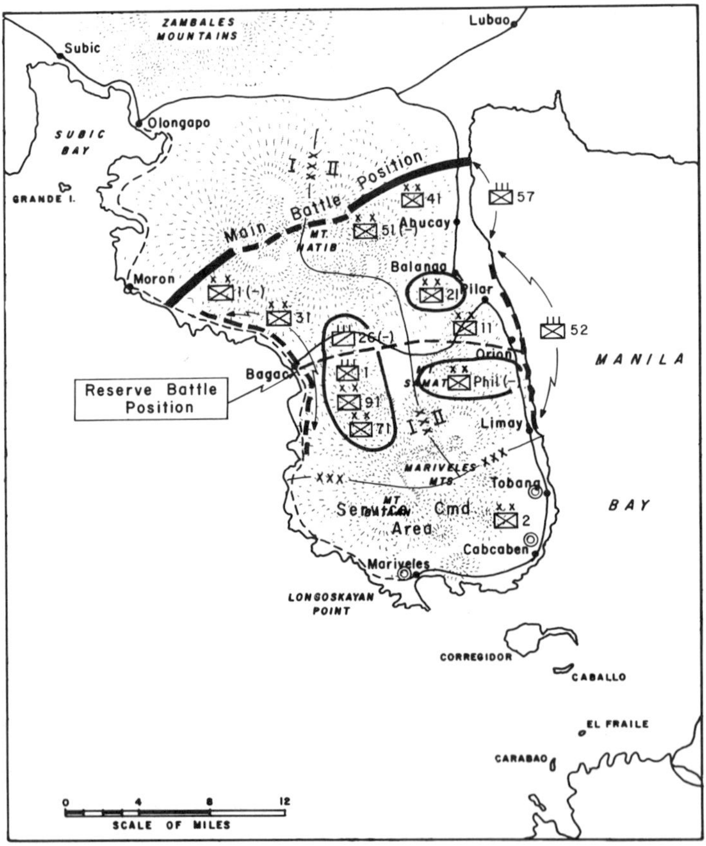

Allied Defensive Dispositions on Bataan, January 1942

thousand of them. It was important that Bataan hold out until the anticipated relief arrived, estimated to be not less than ninety days, and adequate food supplies were essential. We did not have them. As of January 1, 1942, there were sufficient rations to take care of 43,000 persons for ninety days. There were over a hundred thousand, and the first step had to be to cut the rations in half. From the start, those allowances were small, so the cut would make survival barely possible.

The plan for defense was simple: divide all the forces into two Corps, one to take care of the area east of the ridge and another to defend thesection west. The first defense line extended from Abucay through Mt. Natib, thence on to the coast near Moron.. Mt. Natib seemed impassable to the enemy because of its rugged terrain, the absence of usable trails and the extreme difficulty of moving artillery up its slopes and into position for defilading fire. Hence, few troops were assigned to that section. I Corps, under Wainright, was stationed in the western sector and II Corps, under Parker, in the eastern, from the ridge line to the shores of Manila Bay. Our division was stationed near Balanga in the eastern sector, to act as reserves to the 41st and 51st Philippine Army divisions, who were positioned north of us between Abucay and Dinalupihan. The Japanese attacked in our area first, and those divisions held for a few days. But the enemy did the unexpected. They infiltrated up the northern slopes of Mt. Natib with both infantry and artillery, horsed up the slopes part by part, then re-assembled and emplaced, almost without opposition. The main attack had been repulsed and the line held successfully until those enemy troops began to rake our flanks with artillery and mortar fire against which we had no defense. This was approximately the middle of January. Since both the left flank of II Corps and the right flank if I Corps were exposed, it became necessary to ''shorten our lines'', an Army euphemism for retreating still further. The next defense position was established on the northern slope of Mt. Samat, clear across the peninsula and just north of the Pilar-Bagac cross-road. The relative positions of all divisions on the new line were about the same as before.

In scouting for appropriate locations for our batteries, I had a chance for a reunion with Bill Smith, my old friend from Camp Ord. He had been designated a battery commander in the 301st Field Artillery(PA), which was the only heavy artillery unit on Bataan. We had a good couple of hours swapping stories about our experiences to date, and in general conversation about the war. We castigated whomever was responsible for getting us into this mess (including ourselves) and made predictions about what the future might bring—none of the latter were very rosy. I envied his weapons, which were 155 millimeter GPF's, long range guns made by the French. They had been used widely in World War I and were very effective, although difficult to move from place to place. Soldiers called them ''Long Toms.'' Beside them, our own 75's looked like pop-guns. Come to think of it, that's exactly what they were. Bill and I parted with mutual assurances of further meetings, but had no more opportunities for any until the night before the surrender.

Our artillery was emplaced on the east end of the new line near Orion, with the 2nd Battalion on the east flank and the other battalions on our left. We put the self-propelled platoon, one gun on each side of the highway, at the top of a rise that looked down on the plain to the north. They would give us protection against enemy tanks, which were forced to stay on the roads because they couldn't readily negotiate the rice paddies and jungle that covered the rest of the terrain. The other six guns in our unit were placed west of this and could cover portions of the road, in addition to firing on other targets as they were identified by the observation posts. The mounted guns were to be used as close-range antitank weapons and fired on direct line of sight. And it worked out that way; those guns accounted for several tanks during the engagement, a pleasant surprise to those who had been skeptics. Even our own tankers, whose mission we were supporting, liked them.

The rumor mill began to operate overtime again, with less foundation in fact than ever. There were constant reports, purportedly issued by Headquarters, that "Help is on the way", believed implicitly by all for a while, and reinforced every time one of the small ships trapped in Manila Bay changed its position even slightly. We later learned that a large convoy really had left the United States bound for the Philippines. It had been diverted to Australia instead, to protect that country from invasion, and to form the nucleus of a force that could ultimately clear the Pacific again. I still wonder whether that type of rumor was not deliberately circulated in order to keep up morale and preserve the will to fight. If so, it was a very cruel way to accomplish that purpose; the psychological reaction to the truth, when it came, was sad to behold, and spawned a couplet still bitterly quoted by those of us who were there—

> "The battling Bastards of Bataan
> No papa, no momma, NO Uncle Sam"

One of those rumors was typical. It said "on good authority" that a division of our black troops had landed

at Lingayen. They would be used as night-fighters to harass the rear areas of the Japanese army. One is close to the end when he begins to believe that kind of bullshit, and all of us did.

The Japanese came at us again, hard, concentrating once more on the east sector, probably because the roads there were better. The textbooks say that Homma committed only about four regiments, with supplementary tanks, to this attack, expecting that resistance would be light and they would perform only mopping-up operations. Perhaps so, but our own experience was different. The pressure was unrelenting by their ground troops, and was amply reinforced by bombing and strafing from the air. I had thought the earlier attacks were heavy, but the tenacity and ferocity now displayed by the enemy far transcended them. For several days and nights there was little rest, and almost constant artillery and ground action. During the daytime, it was supplemented by the bombing. We ate when we could, mostly cold food, and catnapped during the rare quiet periods. The road was under constant surveillance by Charley, and any movement was likely to bring pin-point artillery fire as well as those bloody bombs. We lost a lot of trucks, and it became necessary to bring up some of the replacement supplies on muleback and by hand-carrying. Nerves were stretched to the breaking point, and the hastily trained Philippine Army began to panic and abandon their lines in greater and greater numbers. Thank God for the Scouts, the tank battalions and the infantry units formed from the excess Air Corps personnel, who were always on the move from breach to breach. They would plug holes left by fleeing Filipino troops, re-establish the lines, then move along to the next troubled area, cursing all the way.

Our own unit was not immune to panic. On one occasion at night, the Japanese infiltrated through the infantry lines and began to surround our gun positions. The first reaction of officers and men alike was to abandon the guns and save themselves. Only the calming effect exerted by Col. Mallonee and Major Bonner prevented what could have become a rout. I'll always be grateful to them for that, and will never quite lose the feeling that I had been tried and found wanting. It was my first personal encounter with the enemy, and for a while I hadn't known what to do about our men, our guns or even myself. I promised myself that such loss of control would never happen again. Fortunately, it didn't.

Panic is caused by the noise and confusion that accompanies unexpected events, occurring under conditions that should not prevail. It is appropriate here to talk a little about how the artillery functions, in order to understand why we reacted as we did. Ordinarily, the light guns are positioned a thousand yards or more behind the infantry lines; larger guns are still further back from the front lines. All of them fire at targets requested by the infantry commanders or by their own observation posts. The key word is "target," a very impersonal term suggesting an object or building that is to be destroyed if possible. Very seldom does the artilleryman think in terms of the people who may be occupying those objects or buildings. It must be the same with the pilots who shoot down other airplanes or who are ordered to bomb factories or the cities around them—persons are not a part of the equation. If it becomes necessary for the artillery to move to the rear, that movement is accomplished under the protective cover of the infantry, who then make their own retreat to new positions. In an ideal situation it may work out that way, but it didn't for us in the incident I described, which caused me so much personal anguish. When my position was about to be over-run, the war became very real indeed and I saw the enemy face to face for the first time. In this case, we were able to establish a good perimeter guard around the guns, and stood fast until the reserves were able to re-form the lines in our front.

I would like to dispose of a myth that all of us shared in the beginning. That concerns the stereotype concept of the Japanese soldier, who was popularly thought to be a bandy-legged runt, buck-toothed, wearing glasses, smiling most of the time and inept. His equipment was supposedly poor and he was considered no match for any American; one of us could take on two or more of him anytime or anywhere, and win. The reality was quite different. We found him to be durable, well-trained, absolutely disciplined, able to fight effectively under conditions that would have discouraged most others, and tenacious to the point of fanaticism. We also learned later that he could be most cruel, insensitive and extremely unpredictable when provoked. His equipment was simple but effective. Japanese society was organized much differently than ours. The people were products of a feudal system which was highly authoritarian, and within which the superior officer had almost unlimited power over his subordinates, including the power of life or death. Their code of behavior was Bushido, the "way of the warrior," which required total obedience and complete abnegation of selfish concerns to what was perceived as their duty to the Emperor. For the military, to fall short of an objective or to surrender to an enemy was unthinkable. Their only failing was that the kind of training they had been given was not conducive to independent thought or action in times of stress, especially in the lower ranks. In spite of that, this soldier was a formidable foe, contrasting strongly with his Filipino counterpart, who had a totally different background and very little training.

The fighting north of Mt. Samat was fierce for about a week or more, straining both sides to their limits. We managed to hold off the enemy, and also to repulse several attempts to land behind our lines on the China Sea coastline. The Air Corps men performed yeoman service there in bloody engagements which further depleted the Japanese manpower and materiel, and they withdrew for a while to regroup and re-supply. It was a relatively quiet period for the rest of February and part of March, during which some changes were made. With the lesson of the abortive landings on the west coast in mind, our commanders concluded that similar attempts could be made from the Manila Bay side and protection was needed there. They ordered new divisional assignments to accomplish that purpose.

The 21st Division was moved from its old position and reassigned to beach defense. Our artillery was augmented by pedestal-mounted guns taken from the ships at Mariveles, which had been stripped of crews for infantry duty, and were no longer of any combat use. Among these was the Canopus, a submarine tender. We were glad to have those odd-looking guns, even though we had to learn how to use them and to train others to do the same. Most were what the Navy called 3-inch, 50 caliber. The bore was three inches in diameter and the length was fifty times that, or one hundred fifty inches. Since three inches is just slightly larger than the 75 millimeter guns we already had, our existing stock of ammunition would fit both weapons. Hendry's battalion was on the north, then Savoie's, then mine in the vicinity of Cabcaben. The infantry were disposed along the whole line, guarding several miles of beach. We used the quiet time for retraining, refurbishing and preparing good gun sites. It also provided time for much-needed rest and rehabilitation for our troops.

Food remained a preoccupation for everyone. Almost all the staples were gone except for a little rice. There were a few canned goods, but we never knew what would be in the cans until they were opened. It could be stewed tomatoes or canned peaches. Rarely was there anything that was solidly filling, but once we did get something that looked promising. It was canned abalone, a muscle that must be pounded to relaxation before being cooked. Otherwise it is as hard as a piece of shoe leather and impossible to chew. The canning factory either forgot that part of the process or the pounding equipment was out of order when our batch went through. Whatever the reason, it was necessary to discard our abalone with no hope of replacement. We had grown to expect that kind of snafu, but it didn't make the loss any easier. The abalone would have been our ration for two days.

Toward the end of February, as the food shortage became more critical, we began killing off the horses and mules belonging to the Cavalry, since the mobility they gave was no longer of any value in our restricted area. The fresh meat was doled out in small quantities to everyone, giving us a significant boost in morale because it was our first solid food in some time. In the States, horse meat would have been considered for use only as dogfood, but there and then it was a delicacy. In fact, all the dogs in Bataan disappeared also, along with snakes and anything else that moved. I thought many times of that *lichon aso* at the *despedida,* almost with longing.

For a while we had some fish. In one of the ammunition dumps were hundred pound bombs, useless now because the planes had been destroyed that could have dropped them on the enemy. We did a very unsportsmanlike thing, and suspended them from bamboo tripods into the shallow waters of the Bay. Each had been equipped with a detonator prepared by the machinists aboard the Canopus, and all were wired together, connected to a battery pack on shore and exploded at the same time. The explosions were muffled but the other results were dramatic: dead fish floating belly-up over as much of the surface as we could see. We harvested many them using small boats, but only a small fraction of the total found its way into the cooking pots. The rest had to spoil because there was no way we knew to preserve it. Oddly, no one thought of smoking, which could have given us a supply lasting many days. I was reminded of the Biblical story of the loaves and fishes, and wondered if those Jews on the shores of Galilee suffered as much from the terrible smell of dead fish as we did. I hoped that the Japanese to our north were as much affected by our home-made gas attack as we were. Bomb-fishing was attempted only once more, on a very limited scale. Otherwise, we depended on small boats fishing surreptitiously at night, and reaping a catch much too small to take care of the needs of both the garrison and the refugees.

All of us felt somewhat detached from what was happening in the rest of the world. We had very little news of the war, and what we did get was vague. Col. Mallonee asked me to go to Corregidor to find out what was happening and to take messages for him that could be transmitted back to the States without compromising security. The messages, I suspected, were merely excuses. What he really wanted was to learn facts about our situation, and that of the rest of the Pacific theater. He felt he needed information which had not been filtered through several layers of censorship and further modified by rumor. I traveled to the island on one of the small boats that sailed twice a day between Mariveles and Bottomside, the port area for Corregidor.

Corregidor is perhaps two miles long and a half-mile wide. The dominant feature is Malinta Hill, toward the eastern tip of the island. West of that is a saddle, then another lower peak looking toward the China Sea. This latter was called ''Topside'', and the large-caliber gun batteries constituting our naval defense were built there. The gun platforms were thick, heavily steel-reinforced concrete, surrounded by a parapet, with ammunition vaults dug into the mountainside behind. The guns were mounted on heavy metal bases topped by hydraulically-operated pantagraphs. When not in use, the gun rested behind the protection of the parapet, and was raised above it for firing by means of the pantagraph. There were several of these emplacements, and the entire installation looked complex and deadly. The guns made Bill Smith's Long Toms look very small; they were either twelve or sixteen inch coastal weapons, more than twice the diameter of his, with a much greater range. Middleside was approximately in the saddle between the two peaks, and contained living accomodations for the peacetime garrison and their families. Bottomside, on the north shore of Corregidor, lay just off the saddle and was the location for the port facilities. The south shoreline of the island had a small port area also, but had been primarily used as a recreational spot for the permanent party and dependents. On the narrow strip jutting eastward from Malinta Hill there wasn't much to see except a landing strip, too short to accommodate anything but small observation aircraft.

I paid only cursory attention to what the other areas had to offer because I was concerned with what I could learn at the headquarters under Malinta Hill. The west portal of Malinta Tunnel was about a fifteen minute walk from Bottomside. The tunnel was driven clear through the hill, slightly up-grade from west to east and was big, approximately twenty feet wide and fifteen feet high at the apex, five hundred feet or so in length from portal to portal. Smaller laterals had been dug at angles to the main tunnel, and were assigned to various activities of the headquarters. One of them was reserved for Manuel Quezon (the President of the Philippines) and his family. Another became the home of MacArthur, with his wife and son, also offices for him and his senior staff. Others were allocated to hospitals, finance functions, personnel, planning, supply, staff quarters and miscellaneous, about fifteen in all. The general atmosphere was totally different from Bataan. For us, the war was very real and ever-present. For most of the strong, well-fed men on Corregidor, it seemed at that time to be merely an intellectual exercise involving the movement of markers an a board as conditions changed. This more or less detached attitude was hard for me to assimilate or appreciate after what we had experienced. I couldn't help being angry at their apparent good fortune—or perhaps jealous is a better word.

Malinta Tunnel and its laterals were not air-conditioned, and relied on natural ventilation, assisted by blowers, to clean out the fumes and odors generated by so many people living so close together. Smoking inside was prohibited. Instead, an area was set up outside the east portal, and everyone who wanted to smoke, including MacArthur, had to use it. I met him there for the first and only time when, close to the end of my visit, I went out to have a last cigarette prior to catching the boat back to Mariveles. There must have been a hundred others in the smoking compound at about four in the afternoon, when the air raid alarm sounded. For me air raids had become a daily occurrence, but for those on Corregidor it was a new experience, and they ran for cover immediately. Dugout Doug was standing at the tunnel mouth, puffing on his famous corn-cob pipe. As each of those tunnel rats (our term) ran for cover, they would have to stop, salute, then run again for protection under the mountain. MacArthur never budged, kept smoking his pipe, and returned all those salutes with flair. I was the last one in because, in spite of the warning siren, no airplanes were yet in view, and I hadn't finished my fresh stateside cigarette. The General calmly flipped me a salute of his own accord, probably recognizing that I was from Bataan, then smiled a little and walked with me into the tunnel. He asked me a few questions, offered some pleasantries and we parted. I was impressed with him, and for that moment at least, was an enthusiastic fan. I have remained an admirer ever since, his monumental ego and imperial attitude notwithstanding. He made some mistakes, but to me, his accomplishments far overshadowed them.

I failed to get the information Col. Mallonee wanted or to send his messages, both for the same reasons, tight security and higher priority radio traffic. I was able to acquire several cartons of cigarettes from a friendly supply sergeant, for me and the other instructors in the regiment. There was also one each for Jesus Cabatbat and Gregorio Mercado.

My trip took place near the end of the quiet period and was followed soon by renewal of Japanese attacks. We knew this was to be the last stand. Our stock of supplies was critically low. There was not enough ammunition any more because most of it had been either fired at the Japanese or blown up in the bombing attacks. Most important, there was no place to go. The enemy was confident and prepared for his final assault, knowing that he was facing a force that was starving and had little left to meet the attack. He had his spies and sympathizers behind our lines, both Japanese and Filipino, who could verify those facts. We knew they were there and did what we could to apprehend and incarcerate them. At first, when we caught someone signalling the location of supply dumps and other installations by mirror flash to the observers flying overhead, he would be taken to the Provost Martial for disposition. However, there were few holding facilities, and most of the ones we took in were released very quickly. Some were able to get back to the front almost as soon as we did. So we quit taking them back to the rear, and it was amazing how many were shot while ''trying to escape.'' I did my own share of that. I hated it and it certainly did not mesh with my Christian beliefs, but the choice between preservation of self and comrades against the life of a traitor was not difficult to make. I had always thought of myself as a reasonably sensitive and caring person, concerned about others and not violent, but this kind of experience forced at least a temporary change in that attitude. Frustration and indignation triggered actions which were totally foreign to me under normal conditions, and which I would like to forget.

9

Surrender

There was a further sharp dip in morale near the first of April, 1942, because of two separate but related events. First, rations were cut in half once more, and half of very little is damn little. It was obvious that nobody could survive for very long on that small amount of food. Second, there had been a change in leadership. In late March, MacArthur was ordered by Washington to relinquish command to General Wainright and go to Australia to take responsibility for the Allied forces building there. This meant only one thing to us: the United States was about to write off the Philippine garrison and concentrate on other priorities. Help was no longer "on the way." It was academic to me because I knew that the end was near. I felt that the unknown we faced could not be much worse than the reality of the present, and had long before lost any feelings of optimism. Most others felt the same, but there was still enough determination left that we would continue to oppose the enemy for as long as possible. It proved to be only one more week.

General Johnathan "Skinny" Wainright moved to Corregidor and took over the leadership of the newly-formed USFIP (United States Forces in the Philippines). His command included all the troops on Bataan and Corregidor, and those Philippine Army divisions in Visaya and Mindanao, which had seen very little action. Everyone in authority knew what the final outcome would be, and it appeared that Wainright had been elected to be the sacrificial goat, but nevertheless he took steps to reorganize his command. He appointed Major General Edward C. King, who had commanded Fort Stotsenberg before the war started, as the top man in Bataan. General King changed some divisional assignments, but our division remained responsible for the defense of the Manila Bay beaches against a flanking attempt by the Japanese. Such an attack was a very real possibility because, if successful, it could end the fight immediately. They had the men, the motive and the materiel, and could commandeer enough boats to transport an attack force across the bay.

It was becoming clear that the Philippine Army infantry could no longer be depended upon to hold their positions against any determined attack. They were deserting to the rear areas in large numbers, discarding their weapons as they went, and the phrase, ''Hey Joe, I go back to join my companions,'' became all to familiar. This erosion became more and more critical as the next few days passed, and we could no longer determine exactly where the front lines were. We knew only that the Japanese pressure was unremitting and resistance to it was fading away. The Philippine Division, the Marines and the Air Corps infantry were committed fully in an attempt to halt the enemy advance, and Hendry's battalion was removed from beach defense to provide more artillery support for them. But these measures were not enough, because there were too many other insoluble problems to meet. By this time, the food shortage was so critical that starvation was becoming apparent, and starving soldiers are simply not capable of sustained violent activity. In addition, the will to continue was disappearing. Savoie's battalion was the first of our units to crack, in spite of their good record. Again, he held them together, this time not by personality and example, but by threats and physical violence. In peacetime it would have been a court martial offense to do that, but here General Capinpin supported Savoie's action strongly, and made threats of his own.

The lines kept retreating southward further, into an ever smaller and more restricted area. Sometime during the night of April fifth, Hendry was ordered to move his guns into new positions a mile or so south. This was accomplished except for one gun whose crew had deserted, leaving Rod alone there. His position was practically in the midst of the advancing Nipponese and adjacent to a forward ammunition storage dump which was being destroyed by our engineers. Shells were exploding all around and the area was an inferno. He stayed there, though, hoping that one of our trucks could get back to him and save the gun. By this time, it was impossible to force any of our native drivers to return to that spot, so Col. Mallonee, Major Bonner and I took a 4 x 4 command car equipped with a towing pintle and drove to where we thought he might be. We found him, quiet and unruffled as usual, but ready to get the hell out of there. It took only a few minutes to get the gun hooked up to the pintle, and we were on our way, exchanging fire as we went with several small groups of enemy soldiers who had infiltrated the area. We were not hit and I suspect that none of them was either, and we made it to the battalion's new position safely. The whole episode was an eerie experience. It was a very dark night, illuminated by the burning ammunition dump and punctuated by exploding shells, with the small-arms fire around us as counterpoint. I suppose the rest were as frightened as I, but too proud to show it. The Colonel, after the war, recommended me for a Distinguished Service Cross on the basis of that night's action.

The following day, nobody knew where the front was and only a few seemed to care. Everywhere there was turmoil. Cars and trucks drove up and down the road without apparent purpose, and dazed foot troops wandered about aimlessly. There seemed to be no coordination and no direction provided by anyone. In the middle of all this, headquarters issued an incomprehensible order—counter-attack!, but only a few made any effort to comply. The general attitude was one of total disbelief; our troops were in disarray, our supplies depleted and there was little to be gained by such a quixotic gesture. At that point, I think almost everyone was prepared to quit.

It happened the next day. Near noon a command car, white flags mounted on each front fender, carried two senior officers forward through our own front into enemy territory. Their mission to was to enter into preliminary discussions with the Japanese on surrender terms, and to prepare the way for the formal capitulation of Bataan by General King. The car returned in a few hours and those officers went directly to his command post to report. We knew some agreement had been reached because action in the front diminished markedly, though it did not cease altogether. Later that night, there was a call for all officers to report to headquarters for instructions. There were close to three hundred of us present, and it was a discouraged assembly in a somber setting. Headquarters was located near the ridge between the two Corps areas. It was in tents, grouped close to the edge of a small clearing in a grove of huge mahogany trees that resembled California's giant sequoias. The night was humid and dark. Those tall trees obscured the sky, and the atmosphere was as gloomy as we. Even the birdcalls were muted. We found a place next to one of the trees and sat with our backs against its trunk, just waiting. We talked very little, not even to speculate about our future.

Finally, after what seemed hours, we were called to attention to greet the General. He told everyone to stand at ease, then proceeded to issue final orders. They were simple and direct. The following day all artillery weapons and mortars were to be rendered useless to prevent their use by the other side. Rifles and sidearms had to be delivered to a central point somewhere south of Cabcaben, by truck, and the rest of our vehicles were to be kept intact and collected together for turning over to the enemy. He ordered that, following this, all troops were to assemble at designated spots by no later than the morning of April ninth, there to await further instructions from the Japanese. Filipinos would be separate from Americans. General King went on to speak of how much our defense had been appreciated by all America, of its value to the war effort and of his confidence in ultimate victory for our side. He complimented various officers who had made outstanding contributions throughout the campaign. We listened without much emotion and there was very little conversation after it was over. There was nothing to say; we had been defeated in the grim struggle, and that was that. As though fated, the meeting was terminated by an earthquake, severe enough to shake those tall trees surrounding us like buggy-whips. There was no noise but the swishing of the tree-tops through the air, and it seemed a fitting climax to a disastrous four months.

We were dismissed and returned glumly to our own bivouacs to plan the disposition of our weapons and other equipment according to orders. It would be a task more difficult than we had first supposed. Getting rid of the small arms and vehicles would be easy, but the guns were a real problem. They couldn't be burned or dropped into the bay, and if dismantled, could be reassembled. Everyone contributed suggestions, the most popular being to shove those guns up the ass of the Japanese; this we discarded as being desirable but impractical. We finally decided to blow them apart, and thus destroy the breech mechanisms and barrels beyond repair. We planned to load into the breech a high-explosive shell with the fuse set at zero delay, then insert another similar projectile into the gun muzzle nose first so that the two detonators faced each other. Then we would attach a long lanyard to the firing linkage so that the man pulling the trigger could be protected by distance and cover from the force of the explosion. With all in place and unnecessary personnel removed for safety, the gunner would pull the lanyard and fire the gun. Gunsights, poor as they were, were to be removed, dismantled and buried. We proceeded on that basis, and after our preparations were complete Mercado and I tried the first one. We did it with considerable trepidation, hoping that our system would function as planned, because if it was not successful we were at a loss for alternatives. It did work, though, and the results were all that had been hoped for; both shells detonated inside the barrel, splitting it for some distance and ruining the breech-block. The other battalions were doing the same, and within a few hours all of the regiment's guns were ready for the junk pile. There were a few misfires, of course, and sometimes we had to repeat the procedure two or three times before achieving the desired end. Those weapons had performed well even though we had cursed them so often, and we felt like we were killing old friends.

While all this activity was going on, I was able to forget for a while the reason for it, and had no time for speculation about the future. But reality crowded in again when the moment came to say a difficult goodby to Mercado, Jesus and other good Filipino friends. Over the months we had developed mutual respect and dependence. We knew it was ended and that we might never meet again. I am aware of no association as peculiarly close as that between members of the same military unit who have been through combat together, and we had shared that experience in abundance. Had I not been too tired, dispirited and worried about what the next day might bring, I might have shed a few tears.

By nightfall Col. Mallonee, Maj. Bonner, Hendry, Savoie and I were walking to the airstrip at Cabcaben, which was our designated assembly point. We travelled light, carrying only a blanket, spare uniform, extra socks, underwear, and a few personal articles, in a canvas musette bag about the size of a lady's cosmetic box. Some wore their World War I type steel helmets but I elected to use only a khaki fatigue hat, which was lighter and more comfortable. We arrived there to find several hundred others already assembled, crowded together for both physical and spiritual comfort but communicating very little. We all knew that a time which had been terrible was over and that another perhaps equally terrible, but perhaps not, was about to begin. Each was buried in his own memories and hostage to his own fears, and everyone appeared to be stretched to the limits of his physical and mental endurance. In any case, we passed a long night—sleeping fitfully when we could, waiting for the dawn and whatever it might bring. We had been told that our own captured trucks would be used to take us to the Japanese internment centers, so many of the men had of their possessions with them, including complete bedrolls and heavy barracks bags.

10

Death March

Eventually morning arrived after that long and restless night, and with it the first of the Japanese under whose control we would be for the next three and a half years. Although many died during those years, I am certain there would have been more if we had known then what faced us, and I could have been one of them. It is fortunate that we have not been given the power to foretell details of the future, because the human mind is not capable of assimilating that much pain at one time.

Humiliation and degradation began with the arrival of those Japanese troops. It turned out that they were not garrison soldiers, but were fresh from what had been the front lines. They felt they had scores to settle and lost no time in initiating the settlement. Orders were barked in Japanese, which nobody could understand and therefore couldn't obey. This triggered the first of the violence which was to become so typical; soldiers moved in with gun butts and bayonets, beating and stabbing those who were slow in forming groups of nearly a hundred men each. I was clubbed once and it was a painful, demeaning experience. We learned the hard way the meaning of the word *Hyaku!* (hundred) and *Kura!* shouted at the top of the voice accompanied by ferocious scowls. More than one who did not understand was bayoneted to death before our eyes. I do not know the precise definition of *kura,* but roughly translated it means that if you are doing something, stop, and if you are not, start immediately. We heard it thousands of times, then and later, and it nearly always meant trouble.

After the groups were formed, the guards began what amounted to a skin search, ostensibly for weapons, but in reality for anything that took their fancy: rings, watches, money, cigarette lighters and anything else attractive. By then, we knew better than to protest. A few of the men had small amounts of Japanese occupation currency as souvenirs, obtained from dead enemy soldiers or Filipino civilians. Those unfortunates were summarily executed, by gunshot or bayonet, without being asked for an explanation or given the chance to defend themselves. While the shake-down was in progress, an interpreter translated a speech by a high-ranking officer to the thoroughly cowed groups. The gist of it was that in their eyes we were not prisoners of war, but captives. (There is a difference between the two; prisoners of war are to be treated in accordance with the provisions of the Geneva Convention, captives have no standing at all). We were to follow orders implicitly, quickly and without question, or receive swift punishment. Having seen examples of that already, we knew he was deadly serious. In addition, he gave us the unwelcome information that we would have to walk out of Bataan. Our trucks would be too busy transporting their men and supplies in preparation for the siege of Corregidor. We would have to march to San Fernando, Pampanga, approximately a hundred kilometers away, where we would be loaded on trains for transportation to an internment camp. That would have been an easy task for fresh, strong troops. We knew it would be very difficult in our weakened, half-starved condition, but fortunately were unaware of the magnitude of that difficulty. This decision was the first of many violations of the agreements made with General King when he signed the surrender documents. The speech-maker said that we would be fed, given a chance to rest and treated well if we behaved. It was a lie, delivered with an extreme arrogance which demonstrated the total contempt the Japanese held for anyone cowardly enough to surrender. Their Bushido code did not permit such action.

We were kept at attention for several hours while combat unit after unit moved southward along the road with equipment of all kinds, including more 240 mm. howitzers than I knew existed. Those weapons were so large that it was necessary to dismantle each one into three horse-drawn sections for transport. The first section was a heavy base-plate topped by a geared steel ring, the second was a massive set of trunnions and the third was the tube and recoil mechanism. This stream of fire-power seemed endless and the gun crews walking alongside their weapons took every opportunity to jeer and strike out at anyone within reach. Our men began to collapse where they stood from heat, hunger, thirst and weariness, bringing a swift reaction from our guards. Thereafter, we tried to avoid more blows by helping each other as much as possible, without much success. I remember one man who broke under the strain, and began to scream and jump around erratically, maddened by the heat, the dust and the brutality of our captors. A bayonet ended his misery.

Finally, there were orders to move out. I thought briefly that it would be a welcome change from inactivity in the baking sun, but it was really no better. We would march for a kilometer or two, then be forced to stand and wait again while more troops passed by. Now the starving men became consumed by thirst, as the little moisture in our systems had long since evaporated. A few men, lucky enough to have a little water left in their canteens, hoarded it jealously, sharing with no-one and allowing themselves only an occasional sip. Once in a while, we passed a small stream or a carabao wallow, but nobody was allowed to break ranks to get a drink or fill a container. The thud of a rifle butt on your back teaches obedience in a hurry. The few who persisted in their attempts to get water were killed and left where they fell. Not until dark was there any further mention of the food or rest we had been promised. Even then there was nothing to eat, and we were told we could fall out and rest by the side of the road, but could not move from there. The Japanese risked no escape attempts, and patrolled both sides of the column constantly throughout the night. Even so, I was so exhausted that I slept soundly on the rocky shoulder, with no blanket or other cushion, just small sharp stones for a mattress. I did not notice the discomfort and neither did anyone else. There were a few who dreamed about the horrors of the previous day, and their nightmare-induced cries could be heard all along the line. No one could help.

The second day was much the same. We marched a short distance then stood in the sun and waited for an hour or so, marched some more and waited again. If there was any shade we weren't allowed to seek it, and I got so I hated the sun almost more than I did the Japanese. The only change on this day was that on one or two occasions some were allowed to break ranks and fill canteens when we passed by a water hole. It didn't matter that it might be covered with scum or have a bloated corpse lying on the bank. Water was water, and possible infection seemed a small price to pay for relief from that terrible thirst. It wasn't a small price. Soon many were gripped by the cramps of diarrhea, but were not allowed to fall out and relieve themselves, so to our other miseries was added the strong smell of feces. It never left us for the remainder of our trek, as dysentery became a normal condition of life. We began to see deaths from exhaustion and sickness added to those caused by the guards, and increasing numbers of men became so discouraged they were ready to quit fighting. I could hear muttering to that effect around me, and it was the first evidence of one of the most frightening phenomena of that whole POW experience, where people could just *will* themselves to die in order to end the struggle. I was determined that it would not happen to me. Life was too precious and the future held too much promise to abandon. I believed this appalling situation was temporary, and began to figure out ways to survive.

It was clear that some of those who were giving up were looking far into the future and could see no surcease from their present agony, hence there was no good reason for continuing. I decided that I would keep my own objectives much closer, and live from moment to moment or day to day. I would make the next step or the next hundred meters, try for the top of the rise in the near distance, but not worry about tomorrow or next month or next year. The next year represented an almost unachievable goal, but the next step did not. I could do that. I began a macabre sort of litany: "Move your left foot, now your right; forget about the water; get to that bend in the road;

don't listen to those guys; we'll get some food tonight, or maybe tomorrow; now take another step, and then one more." It was psychological hype with some elements of self-hypnosis, but helped me get through that day and the ones that followed, and kept me from worrying about a future I could neither anticipate nor control. Emphasis on short-range targets became basic to my survival plan and I used it for the remainder of my years as a POW. I am convinced that dividing long periods into short stretches was one of the major reasons I am still alive and able to write these words, so many years later.

I think it was the third day when we arrived at Limay, where we were herded into the local schoolyard and finally given some food and rest. We hadn't come very far from Cabcaben, but it seemed we had been walking forever. There was water from a tap near the school building, pure elixir for all of us, and all the canteens were filled, though the process took the entire night for our large group. There was also food, unappetizing *lugao,* which is rice cooked into a sort of gruel without salt or other condiment. It was like eating paste with no taste, no body and little food value, except for the weevils which no-one bothered to extract. We were not the first group to pass through there. Someone had dug a slit trench for a latrine, but it was overflowing and the surrounding area was slick with excrement. Our contingent did not improve the situation. Most of the men were afflicted by dysentery and had no bowel control, so relieved themselves wherever they happened to be. The schoolyard quickly became an open cesspool. Instead of showing compassion, the guard force seemed amused and even more contemptuous than ever.

We spent the night there, crowded together in that small space so tightly that there was not room to lie down and sleep. We had to sit with our arms wrapped around our lower legs and our heads on our knees, to doze as best we could amid the cacophony of farts, groans and mutterings all around us. The night had not been restful, and it was a relief to be forced up in the morning, given another serving of that awful *lugao* and set on the road once more. At least the smell would not be so overpowering. On this leg of our journey our steps were shorter, our staggerings more pronounced and the guards more impatient at slow progress. They didn't have to worry so much now that someone might try to escape, because very few were physically capable of that any more. Savoie, Hendry and I started out thin and wiry, but Col. Mallonee and Maj. Bonner were older and heavier, and had used up most of their internal reserves. I was particularly concerned about the Colonel because he was obviously near the limit of his endurance. He began to stagger and stumble, and it was clear that he could not go much further without help, so I relieved him of his musette bag and carried it along with my own for the rest of the trip. That small assistance helped him because he no longer had that weight to carry, and also helped me, because doing it took my mind off my own troubles. At this point, nobody had very much. Those heavy bedrolls and barracks bags had either been discarded early in the first day or confiscated during the shakedown inspection we had before the long walk started. Similar shakedowns occurred at sporadic intervals throughout the entire march, so we had few possessions to worry about.

I still can't remember how many days it took to get to San Fernando. It may have been as many as ten or as few as six. One miserable day blended into another, with nothing to distinguish any of them. We did spend another night in another schoolyard, either at Lubao or Dinalupihan, under conditions very similar to Limay. The harsh treatment slacked off a bit, maybe in part because we had learned a little better how to protect ourselves. For example, I had discovered that one did nothing to attract attention, but tried to stay in the middle of the column and keep moving along. If a person did become noticeable to a Japanese who stayed with the group for any length of time, he was sure to keep coming back looking for an excuse to use his rifle butt on the back or in the groin, seemingly just for the pure pleasure of it. A couple of those blows were all it took to learn the lesson, and my teaching had taken place the first day. Also, as we went further north, the soldiers became less tense and seemed less vindictive and irrational than previously. The guard force kept changing, and possibly the newer units were replacements who had not yet been in the front lines, and consequently were not as bitter and resentful as the earlier ones had been.

At last we shuffled into San Fernando, and few were walking with any vigor. Most, like me, dragged one foot ahead of the other, sometimes not even lifting it from the ground. My socks had rotted away and I was barefoot because my shoes were so painful to wear that I had them hung around my neck by the strings. I would have thrown them away along with the other un-needed items, but realized I might need them later. The guards seemed to relax a little, and did not object too much when the Filipinos who lined the roadside would throw us a small package of food or encourage in other ways some renewed effort. We knew the Japanese had been harsh and repressive with the civilian population, and this was the first time the natives had shown the courage, or had the opportunity to help, and their actions induced the feeling that the worst was over. Our group was herded into a churchyard. The cemetery across the fence could have been a portent of our future.

We had arrived in San Fernando in the middle of the afternoon and were allowed to rest for the balance of that day and the following night. There was more *lugao* to eat, ample water and the churchyard had not been used much before, therefore was reasonably clean. Our stay proved to be only a short respite, because the following morning we were on our way again, a short distance to the railroad yard.

Then began a frightful experience, one of the worst we would see during our captivity. The railroad was a narrow gauge line that had serviced the sugar and rice plantations of the central plain. We were loaded into box-cars with one sliding door each, smaller than the famous ''forty and eight'' French cars of World War I, which had a rated capacity of forty men. The Japanese obviously didn't worry about rated capacity, and like the Filipinos, did not recognize the meaning of the word ''overload,'' or care about its effects on the occupants. They stuffed people into those cars until no more could enter. There was, literally, standing room only for the approximately one hundred men in each car, which had no windows and only one sliding door. When the car was full the door was shut tightly, and another one loaded, until the train was full. In ours, I was packed tightly against a side wall away from the door, and Mallonee and Hendry were close. We could see nothing, and heard nothing but stertorous breathing, curses and the buzzing of ever-present flies. The wait until we got underway was long and the heat intense. There was no ventilation, no room to sit and no room to fall down if a person passed out. Several did, and there was nothing that could be done to help them. Two or three in our car died that way, and most of us did not even know it until the trip was over. If I have any tendency toward claustrophobia, it dates from that experience. The panic and despair were greater than what we had felt on the day the march began, but this time few of us were in physical condition to withstand much more, and the toll was heavier. I have relived that trip in nightmares more times than I care to recall, and it is as vivid today as it was when it happened, over forty-seven years ago. It has been said that the human memory is compassionate, and does not retain the very unhappy and painful things in its storage banks, but does store the good ones for later use in times of stress. I do not believe this myth, because the memories of that horrible trip are still clear to me today, and will be ten years from now if I live that long.

We didn't know our destination, and most of us were too lethargic to speculate about it. After a long day full of starts and stops, the doors were finally opened and we were ordered to come out. The contrast in appearance was shocking. We had gone to the San Fernando station that morning relatively cheerful and optimistic, but the zombies who exited those terrible freight cars were totally different. Cheer, optimism and strength had been cooked out by the heat and foul air, leaving nothing but desiccated shells of men to walk the remaining two miles to the internment camp. We were in Capas, not far from Tarlac, where I had started many months before, and internment was to be at Camp O'Donnell, nearby. O'Donnell would become as infamous as the death march itself, and for very good reasons.

11

Infamous O'Donnell

Camp O'Donnell, located near the outskirts of Tarlac in the province of Pampanga, was originally constructed as one of the training bases for the Philippine Army. It was situated in a shallow bowl bounded on the south side by a meandering creek and on the north by a low hill. Between the creek and the barbed-wire fence surrounding our part of the encampment, there was a narrow dirt road leading west. The American prisoners of war were assigned the easterly section of the base, widely separated by two or three barbed-wire fencerows from the western portion, which was occupied by the Filipinos. The fences created a gap between the two that completely eliminated any chance for inter-communication. Five or six rows of barracks buildings occupied the southeast section of the American compound, and on the north slope sat an isolated group of buildings which were designated by the Japanese as prisoner headquarters, the cookhouse and the "hospital." There was little vegetation, no shade except in the nipa buildings, and only one water spigot to serve several thousand sick and dehydrated people. Between the west fence and the barracks buildings was a large part of the old parade ground, which was very dry and dusty during that Philippine summer. All but the headquarters

Healthiest PWs were selected for group photo. Fort O'Donnell, Death Camp, 15 May 1942, one month after camp was opened.

staff, the cooks and the sick were assigned to the rectangular barracks buildings, each of which could accommodate more than a hundred men. The buildings were all alike, and had double-deck sleeping platforms extending down both of their long walls. There were doors in each and between the platforms, but no common areas. These buildings were the typical nipa construction, built for the Philippine Army, so ventilation was not one of our problems.

On our arrival at the camp, bedraggled and exhausted, we received another of those interminable arrogant speeches by the officer who was in charge. He reiterated many of the harsh regulations laid down to us on the first day of our long walk. Among them were absolute obedience to orders, punishment for any infractions of the rules—especially for any attempt to communicate with civilians outside the fence—promises of food if we behaved ourselves and more threats if we did not. The possibility of escape must have been much on his mind, because one of the first things he did was to group every person into ten-man squads, each member of which was responsible not only for himself, but for the others in his unit. If one man escaped, all the rest in his group would be executed, and if the whole bunch escaped, nine other ten-man groups would be put to death. It had the effect of pitting each of us against all the others, adding mutual suspicion to our woes. If the threat had not been so serious, it would have been amusing, because by now no one had the strength left to even think about escape, much less to try it. That Japanese officer loved to drive through the camp in his American jeep, standing in the back while holding a pole anchored in its floor. He was short, stocky and middle-aged, and one of the few people I ever saw who could strut while standing still. One of the few bright spots in our stay at O'Donnell was the time his driver took a corner too fast, tipped the jeep over and dumped our pouter pigeon on the ground. We thought it unfortunate that he was not hurt. He did lose face though, and relieved his frustration by flailing with his *kendo* stick at everyone in the vicinity.

The 21st Artillery officers, Mallonee, Bonner, Hendry, Savoie and I had managed to stay fairly close together throughout the March and picked bunking spots near each other for mutual comfort. We chose the lower deck on the north side of our building because that side would get the most shade during the day. Friendship was about the only comfort we had, and we had become such good friends that the distinctions of rank were not a consideration any longer. There were other reasons to stay close, among them was that it was necessary for survival. We pooled our meager resources and shared everything. There wasn't much, and the sharing reduced emphasis on our individual selves. It made life a little more bearable.

Our physical condition was deplorable when we arrived at O'Donnell. No one had reserve energy left after

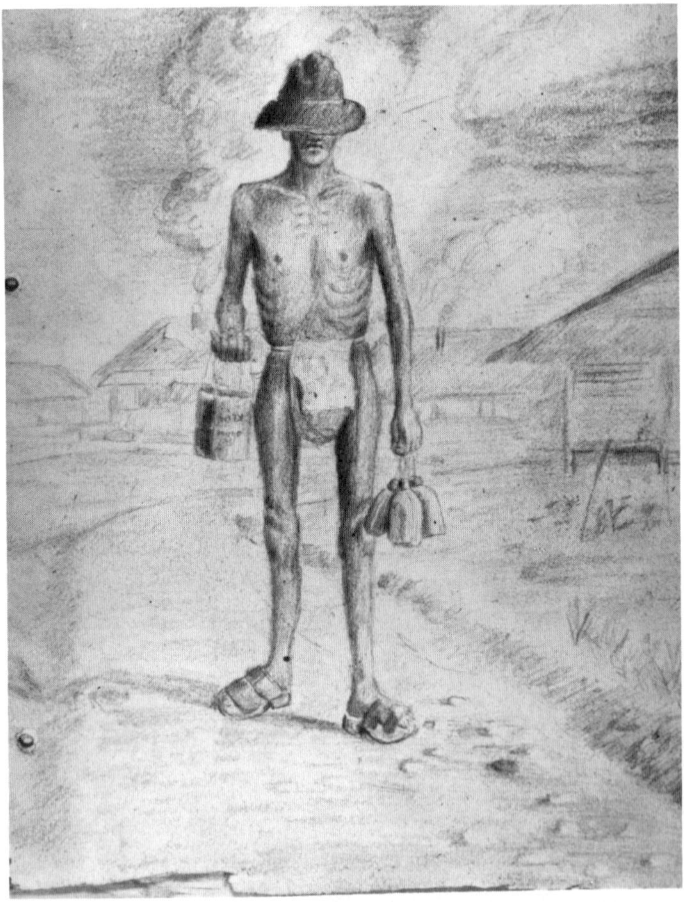

To the Water Spigot

several months of short rations, the trauma of the march and that horrible train ride. Dysentery and malaria were taking their toll, and men were beginning erupt with tropical ulcers (we called them "yaws"), which affected mostly the lower legs and seemed incurable; when one healed another two would appear. The ulcers resulted from infection, and were open sores that suppurated constantly and ate into the flesh, leaving ugly scars in their wake. But our major problems were water and food. There was a lineup at the single water spigot, day and night, all waiting for the chance to fill canteens and to splash the dust off their faces. Each man in the line had several containers, his own and those of his friends who were too weak or too sick to make the effort. It was a slow process, because the water pressure was low and the flow usually a mere trickle. Sometimes our captors would forget to pump water into the supply tank and it would be dry for several hours. That forgetfulness seemed to me like deliberate malice. If so, it achieved its purpose, sowing desperation and discord among those who had to wait and didn't dare lose their positions in the water line. There was never enough to use for bathing or washing clothes, and we limited our consumption to cleaning mess kits, by those who still had the will to do it, drinking and brushing teeth. Water line behavior was not the result of formal rules issued by prisoner headquarters, but was derived from common consent in the solution of a mutual problem.

Food supplies were not much better. Rice was cooked twice a day at the central cookhouse in the headquarters area. It was distributed to the barracks, in partially full five-gallon cans of the type used to carry gasoline—square, with the tops cut off and a wire bail attached.

Sometimes it was *lugao* and sometimes it was cooked so that the rice grains were separate, more palatable but no more filling. There was never enough, and in spite of the different methods employed to assure equal distribution, few could be convinced they were getting their fair share. All such attempts were received with the suspicion that was by now ingrained in us. There would always be bitter comments saying that the next barracks had more in its can than we did, or that one would have a third less in his mess-kit than another. Occasionally, there would be "soup," enough greens floating in hot water to give it a little color, but no food value. Even so, it was wet, and helped to satisfy the craving for water that was ever-present. The Japanese prefer white, polished rice, which they combine with other things like fish, meat and pickles to make up a satisfying meal. Of course, this fare was too good for us, so we got the brown unpolished rice which was considered peasant food. Though not intentional on their part, that substitution probably saved the lives of many, because what food value there is in rice is contained in the husks, not in the white kernel. I'm sure Col. Tsuji would have been indignant if he had known this.

It is still painful for me to describe life at O'Donnell. There was absolutely nothing to do except take care of friends who were sick, swap stories and rumors, speculate on the dubious future, stand in the water line and bury those who had died. There was a so-called hospital, really little more than a charnel house where men were sent to die. As we learned the routine, this became so apparent that the very ill fought transfer by the doctors to that hospital with all the power they possessed, pleading, "Please, *please* don't let them take me there. You know what will happen. If I can only stay here I can get better.

Just give me a little time." Sometimes their pleas were heeded. They died anyway, but ended a little happier because they were among friends.

There were all kinds of ailments. Nearly everyone had diarrhea or dysentery and many had malaria or yaws. Dietery deficiency diseases like scurvy and pellagra began to appear, and there were even a few cases of diphtheria. As many weeks wore on, more and more sickened and died, until finally, fifty or more men a day gave up their lives. The aftermath of death was horrible. Everyone has seen the photographs of the Holocaust, where naked corpses were stacked in piles waiting for burial or other disposition. O'Donnell was the same; the newly dead was stripped of his clothing and other possessions, which were then distributed to the living. His body was carried up the hill and placed on the growing pile near the hospital. Every day the burial detail would dig some more of the ever-lengthening pit, throw in as many bodies as possible, scatter lime over them and cover them up. When there was groundwater close to the surface, it was necessary to hold a body down with your foot while you covered it, otherwise it would float. The stench was overpowering, and the effect on those assigned to the detail devastating. No-one could stand more than a day or two on burial duty, and fortunately there was a rotating roster for that, established by prisoner headquarters. All of us were in such bad shape that there were many instances of people being on the detail one day, and being buried by it the next. All who were able had their turn in the pit, and mine came around a couple of times. I felt de-humanized by those experiences, as did most others. We lost many of the normal mental guidelines that we think of as separating men from animals. Sickness and death in others lost

O'Donnell Funeral

its meaning and compassion for their suffering was only fleeting. We were briefly sorry that it happened but so preoccupied with our own survival that we lost sight of what was happening around us. There were, of course, instances of self-sacrifice and concern for others, but they became fewer and fewer.

In retrospect, I suppose I feel most sorry for the doctors in the camp. There was nothing they could do to alleviate pain or cure an illness. They had absolutely no medicines and could not get them, though they tried and were refused by our captors. A few tried more than once, and were rebuffed again, this time with violence. It seemed that our captors wanted us to die. At that time, this could have been true. In my post-war reading, I learned that at the time Bataan fell, orders were actually issued to eliminate all American prisoners. These orders were drafted in the name of General Homma by a Lt.-Col. Tsuji, a genius as a military strategist but a fanatical *samurai,* who believed that conquered enemies should be eliminated. Subordinate commanders refused to execute those orders until they came from General Homma himself. When he learned of their existence, Homma rescinded them, but by that time much damage had already been done. In any event, the doctors were helpless to offer anything more than encouragement and the comfort their words could give, which didn't save many lives.

Chaplains were as helpless. Gatherings were not permitted except in the privacy of the barracks, and opportunities for holding services were curtailed almost to the vanishing point. A few tried an informal kind of meeting while standing in the water line, but without much success, because the fixation on getting water was too great to allow for outside distractions. Like the doctors, the chaplains were limited to personal contacts, providing some comfort to the dying and attempting to give to the living a spiritual reason for continuing the fight for survival. It was a losing battle.

Before we had been in this camp for very long, the colonels and generals were separated from the rest of us and taken to some other location. Mallonee was among them. Those remaining resented that, because we felt they had been singled out for preferential treatment, and considered it an unfair example of "rank has its privileges." The suspicion of senior officers ingrained in every soldier played a part in that resentment. In O'Donnell it was more complicated because life was so harsh that selective improvement for anyone caused a bitter reaction. It turned out that our adverse judgment was unwarranted. I learned after the war that they were sent to separate facilities, first in Formosa and then in Manchuria, but their treatment in those places was little better than ours.

The Filipinos interned in the area west of us fared worse than we. Part of my daily routine was to walk the perimeter fence as far as I was able. It gave me some exercise and removed me from from the depressing atmosphere of the barracks for a while. Sometimes I would go alone, but I was often in the company of my friends. In the beginning, we favored the west and south fences since they were the farthest away from the hospital and burial ground. It lost its attraction after the first few weeks because so many Filipino deaths had occurred that their original cemetery was full, and a new one somewhere to the south of us was opened. Day after day they passed by down the road between the fence and the creek and disappeared around the bend, sad processions of body after body. Each was in a blanket suspended by its corners from a pole carried by two men, and we counted as many as four hundred in one day. I think it was this terrible attrition that finally convinced the Japanese they had to take some action. We thought the Americans did not matter to them, but knew that, in order to occupy the Philippines, they must somehow secure the co-operation of the Filipinos. For them to do this, the carnage had to stop, and the only way to accomplish that objective was to free the remaining Filipinos, move the Americans to some other location and close O'Donnell. This they did, about three months after our arrival. But it was too late to save the thousands who had died there and much too late to establish the reputation of beneficent conquerors they so desired.

Whatever their reason, O'Donnell was closed and we were moved once more. This time we were transported, in the American trucks we had been forced to abandon in Bataan, as far as the railroad station at Capas, which was several kilometers away. There we were loaded again into those tiny box-cars, but they were not too overloaded and the doors were left open. Thus, we made the trip, if not in comfort, at least under tolerable conditions. It was a good thing, too: very many would not have made it otherwise. Our destination turned out to be near Cabanatuan and was another training base they called Camp No. Three, in the eastern part of the central plain of Luzon, Province of Nueva Ecija. The reasonably comfortable ride, and entry into a comparatively clean area, gave me hope that the worst was over and I might be able to survive a little longer. The nightmare of the March and of O'Donnell was behind us. What lay ahead, none could foretell. We knew only that it might be better, and couldn't be worse.

12

Cabanatuan

Camp Three was near the town of Cabanatuan, one of the major population centers in the province of Nueva Ecija. The camp layout was similar to the one in O'Donnell, with rows of nipa barracks, a parade ground and an administration area. The buildings had been occupied before for a short time by the Philippine Army, and were clean and relatively fresh. Again, there were few trees, but there was sufficient open area that one could walk and exercise in comparative privacy and without fear of stepping into something unspeakable. The barbed-wire fence was there, as well as guard towers set at intervals around its periphery. The guards themselves, though ever-present and unreasonable, were not the cruel savages we had faced before. There were many restrictions on our activities, and the Japanese command whimsically changed them from time to time, often without notice and always without explanation. Even so, Camp Three was a paradise compared to our previous experiences. The surrounding area is agricultural, as it was then, and supplemental food could be obtained from the Filipinos if one had money or trading materials. Very little of it came through the fence as a compassionate offering. There was plenty of water available for the three or four thousand men who were forced to live in Cabanatuan. We could use it for washing as well as cooking and no longer had to wait in those interminable lines at a spigot.

Perhaps the most important difference was that the new camp had an established and functioning POW organization. The commanding officer was US Marine Lt.-Colonel Beecher, stocky and arrogant as only a Marine can be, but obviously in charge. He was a stickler for sanitary discipline. The areas had to be kept as neat as possible, and new latrines dug and ready before the ones in use were full. Kitchens were cleaned after each meal and personal hygiene was stressed. He was also strong on military courtesy and did much to re-establish the practice, if not the spirit, of that system. Each barracks had its officer in charge. There was even a sort of military tribunal which mostly confined itself to adjudicating personal disputes. Occasionally, violations of Japanese camp regulations were resolved internally which could have resulted in severe punishment of the offenders by our captors had they known of them. Colonel Beecher had detractors who resented his high-handed methods, and spread rumors that he lived high while others suffered—that he never seemed to go hungry, remaining healthy-looking while the rest of us were starving. Despite these complaints, he positively influenced our mode of living, and that was good for everyone. His emphasis on sanitation and grooming saved lives over the long run, and he helped to re-instill the pride that had been so badly shattered. I resented him for his attitudes, yet admired him for the results he achieved.

When you reach the point where even a slight improvement in food, sanitation or other physical condition seems to be sheer luxury and any change at all is for the better, it is amazing how the human spirit rebounds from the depths of despair to renewed hope. So it was with us. Cabanatuan Camp No. Three had not been used as the kind of way station that O'Donnell had, and was comparatively well-organized. Those already in residence there had come from Corregidor after its fall on May 8, 1942. They had been transported by truck from Manila, and were therefore in much better condition than we. They had established civilian contacts, and started black market operations that ultimately added to the total food supply of the camp, though at high cost to the recipients.

These men from Corregidor resented the veterans of the Death March for many reasons. We were filthy, having had no baths for months. We were sick, carried with us the seeds of infection and disease, and were undisciplined. Respect for the authority and rank of superior officers had been ground away by the terrible experiences of the march and of O'Donnell until we were a rag-tag mob, unruly and cynical. We had no trading materials because all those had been confiscated months before. In sum, we represented a threat to the way of life they had established which, though unpleasant, had been much better than ours. We also resented them. We were paranoid and envious, regardless of the relatively small differences in our circumstances. We realized that if any of us were to survive, the burden of change would fall on our own shoulders, and the knowledge rankled.

Life at Camp Three was no bed of roses, even with the improvements forced by Col. Beecher. Sickness was still rife and many were dying, though the rate declined gradually from that at O'Donnell. Food rations were so short they would barely sustain life. They consisted of unpolished rice sweepings, mixed sometimes with barley and always with maggots and worms. We hardly ever bothered to remove the latter, considering them a potential protein source. There were soups almost every day, the same sparse vegetable greens floating in hot water. Once in a while there were mongo beans, but these came so seldom and in such small quantities that they added little quality to our diet. The limited food supplies that were issued made assignment to cooking in the kitchen a very coveted detail. We rarely saw a thin cook. Somehow they always managed to end up with a double or triple portion of the usual food plus many of the extras, like mongo beans, that were delivered to the camp. Officers, other than the man in charge of the kitchen, were not assigned as cooks and never allowed by the Japanese to volunteer for that duty. The same restriction was also true for the other work details, except for farming. Any job that involved contact with the outside world was performed by enlisted men, who reaped such rewards as there were, but it deepened the chasm between them and their offi-

cers that is normal even in garrison life. In our situation, that natural antipathy was exacerbated by the fact that otherwise we lived, ate and did everything else in close proximity. It was a reversal of the old saying, ''Rank has its privileges.'' In Cabanatuan, lack of rank carried the privilege.

Next to food, the biggest problem was the huge blue-bottle flies, which bred by the millions in the open latrines throughout the camp. They were everywhere. They invaded our barracks, and found their way into our noses, eyes and ears, even into our mouths if we opened them more than a minimum. It took constant effort to keep the flies away from our food for long enough that we could eat it. We would take a bite and wave them away, another bite then more waves. We were not always successful and most meals involved eating at least a few. I still gag at the thought of that, and am convinced that much of the energy derived from the poor food was expended in shooing the flies away. It became so bad that a campaign was instituted in the attempt to eradicate them. For each hundred flies killed there was a small reward, like an extra Japanese-made cigarette. Everyone participated and we smoked more, but didn't make much of an impact on the fly population. They multiplied faster than we could control them. There was an increase in the number of malaria cases, because we were also plagued by mosquitos, which are carriers of that disease.

Still, we lived better than we had before. We could wash our clothing and take an occasional sponge bath in tap water. Sometimes, we could do both at the same time as the tropical rainstorms swept through the area. Being clean again was the ultimate luxury after those months of living like pigs, and did more for our morale than any-

Wash Day

thing else could possibly have done. We were able to shave and get a marine-type skinhead haircut, which reduced the infestation of fleas. These improvements did much to restore the pride we had lost at O'Donnell. Our better life also restored the desire to converse about something more than our own troubles, and we gradually began to learn what had happened in the world during our isolation. That knowledge was interesting, but not particularly encouraging. It was an almost unbroken tale of defeat and retreat on all Pacific fronts by our side and of ever-expanding conquest by the Japanese. The Greater East Asia Co-prosperity Sphere had become a reality, except for Australia, and the enemy were in the process of consolidating their gains.

It was mid-summer then, and we finally learned what had happened to Corregidor after the fall of Bataan. General Homma had lost no time in moving his troops and artillery into position along the southern shore of the peninsula. The enemy had emplaced an almost unbroken line of those heavy howitzers we had seen, stretching eastward along the coast of Bataan from Mariveles. They immediately opened a continuous barrage against the whole island, and it was very effective. When the island surrendered on May 8th, one month after Bataan fell, all the surface installations had been destroyed, and even the vegetation was gone. Apparently, each gun had been trained constantly on a particular spot, and any movement in that area resulted in an instant fusillade. Surrender had been inevitable, but this bombardment accelerated it. Finally General Wainright was forced to ask for peace talks. His intention was to surrender only the island fortresses, but the Japanese insisted the Visayan and Mindanao garrisons be included, so that the entire USFIP would have capitulated at the same time. To avoid further bloodshed and protect the civilian population as much as possible, Wainright finally agreed and the enemy became the undisputed masters of the Philippines.

Those from Bataan had harbored the feeling that we had failed, but we found instead our effort was not in vain. The Japanese had established a timetable, allowing about fifty days from their first landing to complete the conquest of the Islands. That would have permitted them to stage their assault troops south for an early invasion of Australia. By then, Singapore and Malaysia had already fallen, as well as Indonesia. The four months it actually took to subdue us cost them the opportunity to attack Australia, since it had allowed the Allied forces time to begin a massive concentration of forces there. This materially decreased Japanese odds for a successful outcome and their projected invasion was deferred, permanently.

We had been concerned about the fate of the nurses, and were much relieved to find they had been evacuated to Corregidor at Bataan's fall and remained there as long as that fortress lasted. Then they were moved to the Santo Tomas University campus, the internment camp for civilians near Manila. Apparently they had not been harmed. The patients at Field Hospitals One and Two in Bataan were not so fortunate. The enemy had made an unprovoked bombing attack on Hospital Number One, and caused many casualties, both killed and wounded. Those survivors who were ambulatory had been forced to begin the March along with the rest of us, but few of them completed it. Some of the bed-ridden patients had been killed and others remained there for a while, but nobody knew their present whereabouts. I have never found out what happened to them.

Other topics were soon exhausted, among them the relative degree of heroism displayed and deprivation undergone by either the Bataan or the Corregidor defense forces. Claims and counter-claims were bandied back and forth at a great rate, but it was the kind of argument neither group could win. We knew it so went on to other subjects such as food. A favorite was, ''When will the Americans get off their ass, get over here and take us out?'' Rumors abounded again as they had so often in the past, and with even less foundation in fact. This time though, we regarded them more as entertainment than news, and vied with each other to see who could start the most outrageous tale, how fast it could circulate through the camp and in what form it would return to the originator. We even got up pools on outcomes. In retrospect, all this seems to me to have been a little childish, but I suppose it really wasn't, because there was absolutely nothing to read and no dependable source of verifiable news. Gossip represented a relief from boredom.

The Japanese allowed other activities to pass the time inside the fence. I presume they thought if we were otherwise occupied, there would be less trouble for them, and they were probably right. For a while, there was baseball, not continued for very long because none had the energy to pursue it. We did have some theatrical performances, more or less successfully, but the best entertainment was furnished by a few of the men from Corregidor who were musicians and who had been able to bring their instruments into Cabanatuan. I remember with particular pleasure three of those: a guitarist, a saxophone player and a man who cobbled together a set of drums. Together with a few singers they gave some great concerts. The music was good, but its reminders of home left us all nostalgic and pensive. There were also song-writers and poets, whose outpourings were usually not high-quality, but each had a message with meaning to us. I copied one of the poems into a small school notebook and brought it home with me. The author is unknown to me, but because he has caught the essence of prison camp life in such graphic detail, it is included here.

Prison Camp Elegy

There are things about a prison camp
That I don't like, no bedside lamp
For reading nights, the lack of books,
The rough and over-bearing cooks
No privacy, no private places
The close-cropped heads and hairy faces
The tasty food that's always missing
The diarrhea and non-stop pissing
The fact of calling Pesos 'P's
The absence of big mango trees
The acrid smoke of galley fire
The all-enclosing Jap barbed wire
The loud and almost ceaseless chatter
Of little men who do not matter
The maggots, flies and dripping rain
The sale of medicines for gain
Some heroes of Corregidor
Whose bravery grows more and more
With every time they glibly tell
Of how they spurned each bomb and shell.
The rumors that are daily rife
In fact, I hate the whole damned life
Our chow deluxe or sardines tinned
The smell that comes with each west wind
The sniping of our cigar butts
From dirty gutters 'round the huts
The athlete's foot and dhobi itch
That pretty phrase, "You son-of-a-bitch"
For months we've fed on rice and greens
With now and then some mongo beans
And dream of meals at Jai Alai

With all the food that cash could buy
For months we've slept on ground or floor
And waked each morning stiff and sore
At night we rise six times or eight
From bed to run and urinate.
For months we've had no news but scuttle
Or Japoganda most unsubtle
We don't know if the Yanks are landing
Or if our captors are disbanding
For months we've listened to Army slang
Fouler that the jargon of an East Side gang
Been ordered around by an upper-ranker
With an IQ minus or even blanker
But it won't be long now, it can't be long
now
Before we'll never see lugao
Or have to supplement our chow
With purchases from army truckers
The lousy, profiteering suckers
Before we sleep in cosy nests
On eiderdowns or Beautyrests
Beside some woman warm and sweet
Away from snores and stinking feet
Before we'll quit this bloody pissing
Indulge instead in luscious kissing
Look once more the well-dressed mister
And not an animated blister
Before we'll never want for rain
To wash away the dirt and stain
Of sweat and mud and sticky clay
Accumulated day by day
And lose the God-damned blue-arsed flies
That foul our annual chocolate pies

Get relief from rain and heat
And use a normal toilet seat
We'll soon stop all this sort of thing
As guests of Nippon's Sun God King
No longer we'll salute and bow
The Yanks are back in Mindanao
Guerillas roam the countryside
(Unless our very ears have lied)
In thirty days or some weeks more
We'll be the guests of Ecuador
Or, spreading it a little thinly
We'll leave forthwith for Fort McKinley
And God knows we soon must leave the
    Army
Before we go completely barmy
Maddened by the pricks diurnal
Of a tunnel-squatting Colonel
Soon we'll leave this Bangabong
It can't be long, It can't be long.

This saga of sadness inspired an answer, again by an unknown author, expanding on the first complaints, and is appropriately entitled:

Addenda

Oh friend, your plaintive late lament
Has reached a sympathetic ear
And fanned to light an urge to vent
A few more deprecations here.
It irks me sore to be addressed
By Nippers as "the Emperor's guest"
And directed here and there by grunts
From bandy-legged little runts.

I'm sick of rice, tasteless and flat
With foreign bits of this and that
Contributing contamination
That won't invite examination.
I'm tired of calling meals a ration
Of campaign hats worn cowboy fashion
Tired of soggy, muddy boots
Of hill-billies in soldier suits.
Of groping in the dark at night
Of getting up before it's light
To face a barren empty day
Of trying to fill it in some way
With idle, futile, ceaseless choring
Cares or pastimes just as boring
Adorning mess-kits, for example
This lousy poetry's a sample
I'm tired of going without meat
Of sitting on a still-warm seat
Of flies that hatch from maggots there
That soar and buzz 'round bottoms bare
Of seeing sores on arms and legs
Of shaven pates as bald as eggs
Tired of someone's tuneless whistle
Of wild-hair beards that droop or bristle
Of acheing back and raw-rubbed hips
Serrated by the bamboo strips
Tired of childish, loud discussions
Tired of rectal repercussions
Malodorous, oleaginous ones
Resounding through the night like guns
I'm tired of hearing men called "Joe"
Of dividing all things just so
Of splitting seven spoons of stew
One for me and one for you

Of endless lines on every hand
Where eternally I'm forced to stand
At muster, chow, early and late
And even when I defecate
Everything I want or do
A thousand others want it, too
Fed up with all the constant blowing
Of hero crop that's daily growing
Who speak of Tunnel Rats as "They"
When "We" is what they ought to say
Tired of wierd, yardbird gyrations
And officers' puerile machinations
To look out for number one
Of an Army that seems to think "civilians"
Is a term synonymous with "millions"
Tired of rumors varied, diverse
Peddled by omniscient drivers
Of scuttle-butt without surcease
Sick of trying to solve the riddle
Of getting up at night to piddle
Tired of the muddy trail we tread
On nocturnal visits to the head
Of seeing hopes of night
Come crashing down at morning's light
To this vapid, miserable existence
I fast am losing my resistance
I'm tired of the motley multitude
That daily I must see
And if you ask each one of them
You'll find they're just as tired of me.

Written at Cbanatuan POW Camp Three
Cabanatuan, Nueva Ecija, P. I.
August, 1942

Who could say it better, or with more feeling?

Just when I thought things were getting better and that I would make it through these trials, something happened that made me hope I wouldn't. I contracted hepatitis, or yellow jaundice. It was the most nauseating, painful experience I have ever had, and embarrassing because one of its effects was the loss of all bladder control. There was no medicine, so one of the POW physicians told me the best thing I could do was to eat all the sugar I could get my hands on. After some trouble I managed to get a small supply through the fence. It was raw and brown, and I consumed as much as possible at a time as often as I could, until the very sight made me even sicker. I continued the treatment through two or three miserable weeks and several cycles of severity. Finally, the disease abated and I returned to normal, although I didn't lose my ghastly yellow color for a month or more. The most notable result of all this has been that I still can't look at any kind of sugar without getting queasy, and haven't used more than a spoonful deliberately in the forty-odd years since the war ended. It hasn't been all bad though, no one has been willing to accept a blood donation from me in all that time, for fear of contamination.

There were two camps at Cabanatuan, No. One and No. Three. By mid-September, the attrition rate at both had been so high through death and the dispatch of work groups to various parts of the Islands that the Japanese decided to consolidate them into one unit. It was to be located at Camp One, just a few miles away from us. So, near the end of the month, Camp Three was closed and we moved once again. The new situation was much the same as before: poor food, little to do, nothing to read—little exercise for mind or body. Again we were the interlopers, and had to experience the same kind of suspi-

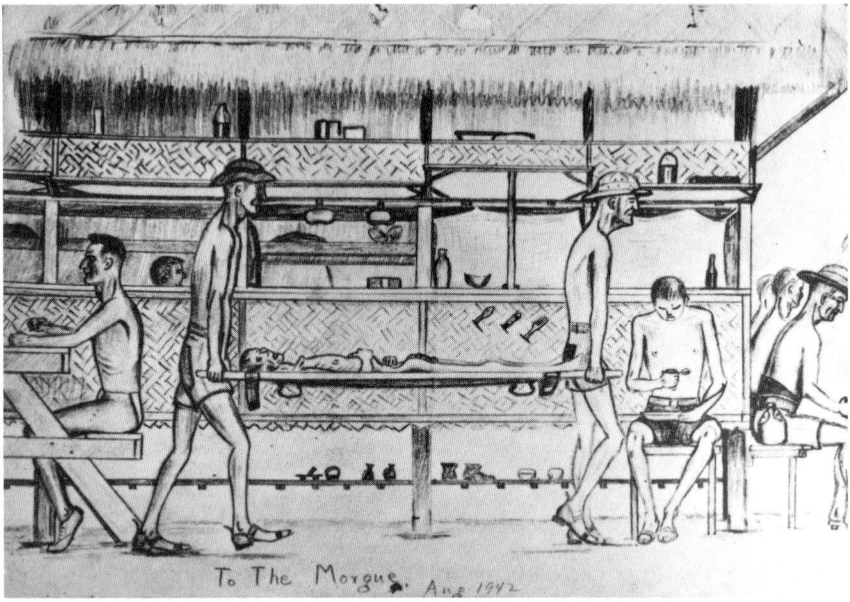

Funeral Procession

Interment

Minor Punishment

Major Felony

cion and resentment we had seen initially in Camp Three. Col. Beecher was appointed as Commanding Officer of the Prisoners almost immediately, and continued in his authoritarian ways. We were used to them and by now convinced his basic goals were correct, though we disliked his methods as we had MacArthur's at the start of the war.

The Japanese decided that the camp should become self-supporting, grow its own food, collect its own wood for the fires and do all the other things necessary to maintain itself. Those who did not already have work assignments, such as truck drivers, wood gatherers or special details of many kinds, were sent to the farm plots allocated to us in the vicinity. It was hard work for debilitated men, and there was little chance to acquire extras like food or medicine, but it did get us out in the sun with a purpose. This was good for both minds and bodies that had been unused for several months.

It provided nothing in the way of food for me, because before the month ended I became one of fifteen hundred men who were selected to go to Japan early in November. Previously, work details had been sent to other locations on several occasions to build airstrips or do other manual labor. Those chosen for our group were the healthiest remaining at Cabanatuan, so we knew we also would be required to work. I did have a chance to see most of my Salt Lake friends, as well as others who had become close to me, before we departed. Each time we separated we waid good-by, knowing that the probability of seeing each other again was small, and those farewells were poignant.

13

The XX Maru

As our convoy moved away from Camp One, there were mixed feelings in those left behind. On one hand was the pain of losing old friends and on the other relief at having the camp less crowded and, as a consequence, the possibility of larger rations. The latter turned out to be a vain hope. The population was certainly reduced, but so were the food issues, and I have been told that they did not improve until about the first of the year 1943. For those of us who departed, there was some hope for the future. We would be moving out of the war zone and its pressures, away from the tropical diseases which had affected so many and into a situation that might be better. Optimism is hard to suppress.

The convoy rolled through the streets of Manila past throngs of its native residents, many of whom surreptitiously flashed the ''V for victory'' sign. Few had the courage to call out good wishes and many seemed shocked at our emaciated appearance, but we did sense good will and encouragement. The trip through the city did not take very long. We entered the Port Area, dismounted from the trucks and marched onto the dock to behold the sorry ship on which we would travel to the Japanese homeland. It was a rusty old bucket, a singlestacker of about five thousand tons displacement, which hadn't seen a coat of paint in years. The bridge structure, containing the control center and quarters for the crew and VIP passengers, was amidship and there were cargo holds surmounted by derricks both fore and aft of that. The "head," or latrine, was aft on the starboard side, a framework built out over the rail so that bare bottoms would be exposed to the wind and weather and the droppings fall into the sea. Not all of them had, and there was an ugly brown stain all the way down the side to the water line. The ship had a name painted on the bow, but it was nearly obliterated by time and the elements. I have found since that it was *Nagato Maru*. All Japanese ships are the something *Maru*, meaning ship. As the voyage progressed it turned out to be a hell ship, but my feelings toward it far transcended that simple expression, so I will call it the *XX Maru*. If *XX* represents the most profane and ugly expressions that come to mind, it will give a close approximation of my feeling for that tub. The initial shock of its decrepit appearance and ripe odors began to erode away much of the optimism we had so carefully, and mistakenly, developed.

The prisoners of war were herded into the aft hold. There were fifteen hundred of us crowded into space designed for far fewer than that. The hold was fitted with temporary sleeping shelves, in tiers three or four high, built from the stern forward to the bulkhead separating the hold from the engine room. The sleeping bays surrounded a small open area, where there was a ladderway up to the hatch opening. We were crowded into these tiers so tightly there wasn't room for everyone to lie down at once. In the beginning we all sat, but one can't do this continuously through three weeks on the ocean, so we developed a system of shifts wherein half would sit or stand so the other half could recline. It didn't matter whether you were sitting or reclining, because there wasn't much rest to be had. The platforms were made of rough bare planks with no covering of any kind. We had no blankets, and used our virtually empty musette bags as pillows. The lack of padding was extremely hard on bodies so thin that knees, hipbones and ribs showed clearly through almost translucent skin. Though we were accustomed to stench, this time it was compounded. The hold had been used recently to transport horses and their residual odor, combined with the human smells, was close to unbearable.

As soon as the last man was below deck in the hold, the Japanese crewmen covered the opening and battened the hatch cover down. Then there was no fresh air at all and the heat buildup in tropical Manila harbor was immediate and severe. There were no portholes and no light, and men whose internal strengths were already strained now began to panic. We had been selected for this detail because we were the "healthiest." That was only a relative term; everyone was in marginal condition and many were sick with dysentery, malaria, tropical ulcers or a combination of the three. It was the latter who began to lose control first. Some screamed and threshed around and had to be physically restrained from doing themselves harm, but nothing could stop the noise, and that hold became bedlam. Of course the panic soon spread to others. The Japanese crew had placed a couple of five-gallon cans in the open space for use as latrines. They were grossly inadequate, like everything else provided, and were soon overflowing. The deck, and even the sleeping bays, took on the same appearance we had seen

The XX Maru Hold

at Limay and Lubao: slimy, odorous and disgusting. The Black Hole of Calcutta could not have been worse. Many tried to climb the ladder and plead with our captors for relief, but there was no response except shouted orders understood by none, and threats understood by all.

Finally, the ship began to move slowly through Manila Bay toward the open sea. After two terrible hours the hatch cover was removed, and a few men were allowed on deck to use the head. I was among them, and had the opportunity to see Corregidor as we passed. The island was far different from my memory of it. In confirmation of the stories we had heard in Cabanatuan, it was barren and brown, a great contrast to the lush beauty we had observed from the Cleveland a year earlier and that I had seen on my visit there the previous March.

Though the hatch cover was off and there was some light in the hold, the crew did not rig an air scoop for ventilation, so conditions below-deck improved very little. The madness caused by heat and close confinement continued, and people fought for the chance to get on deck. Not all could, and restraint by the Japanese once more included the use of rifle butts and bayonets. Those who succeeded found that in addition to the POW group, there were a few hundred Japanese soldiers being returned home, who were quartered in the forward hold. There was also a deck load of damaged airplanes and artillery pieces going back for repairs. No markings of any kind distinguished the ship as carrying prisoners of war, so we were fair game for any submarine that might be in the area. This was a clear violation of the rules of warfare, which require clear marking of prison ships and prohibit dual use of them for military purposes. It was one of many such transgressions committed by the Japanese during the war. They had never ratified the Geneva Convention regarding treatment of prisoners and used that to their own advantage on many occasions to our continuing detriment.

The *XX Maru* cleared the entrance to Manila Bay and turned north into the China Sea on its way to Formosa and then Japan. The first few days of the voyage were uneventful except for the continuing physical and mental trauma suffered by everyone. I shared bunk space and reclining shifts with Alan Cory, an infantry major, and Jim Baldwin, a lieutenant in the transport service, and we whiled away the long hours swapping tales of home and our previous experiences. Cory was a Texan who had settled in Tulsa, Oklahoma and he loved to talk. In civilian life, he had been an ice cream manufacturer and felt that ice cream, next to beef and potatoes, was the most essential and the most interesting of all American foods. I learned much more than I wanted to know about ice cream: its ingredients, their proportions, the exact sequence of mixing, how to assure the correct air content. We discussed flavor preferences of the public, marketing methods and distribution systems—the whole nine yards. We even talked seriously of how to go about making and selling ice cream fritters, if you can imagine that. Alan was nearly as enthusiastic about Texas as he was about his business, and long monologues about his home in San Antonio and the glories of the rest of that state were quintessentially Chamber of Commerce propaganda. It was overkill, and I made up my mind never to live there if I could possibly avoid it. But he was a good man and our long, though one-sided conversations helped to mask the miseries surrounding us for a few hours at a time.

Jim was equally interesting, but not as verbal. He was originally from my home state of Utah, but had moved with his parents to the Philippines several years before the war, and they had been successfully operating a shipping firm, Macondray & Co., Inc. He knew a great deal about ships and commerce, and could tell some fascinating stories about the intricacies of conducting business in the Orient. Politics and bribery, especially in the Philippines, was a fact of life as necessary for success as good accounting or good equipment. Bribes were paid to all authorities, from the customs inspector at the dock to the President of the Republic. Jim told stories of lavish poker parties aboard the presidential yacht to which aspiring businessmen were invited. None of them refused these invitations and their losses were invariably heavy. Quezon must have been a consummate poker player because no one but himself ever won. Jim also knew our ship, which had been sold to the Japanese well before the war to be scrapped as junk, and though it had not been scrapped, was still junk.

In spite of the welcome distractions provided by my two companions, it was impossible to ignore what was going on around us as the ship made its slow progress northward. Conditions had become worse. Dysentery was rife, and fewer each day could make it up to the head on deck. The result was an ever-deepening pool of filth around those five-gallon buckets at the foot of the ladder and in the bays themselves. Men alternately sweated and shivered with the hot and cold cycles of malaria. Incurable ulcers opened and spread. The panic of that first day abated somewhat and was replaced by a terrible, deadly lethargy; several bodies went over the side each day, after a perfunctory burial ceremony and with little compassion shown by the Japanese. There must have been some food issued, but I do not remember it. I do remember the lack of water vividly. There was so little to drink that many were crazed by thirst and even tried to drink their own urine. A few did other unspeakable things just to obtain some kind of moisture. For example, there was an incident where one man attempted to cut the vein in the arm of his sick neighbor in order to drink the blood. He was barely stopped in time to prevent that by those nearby. Some never recovered from the psychological impact of that appalling trip. It is difficult now, in the comfort and security of my own home, to believe the things I have described really occurred—but they did.

It took several days to get as far north as Formosa, and the weather was getting worse. A typhoon developed that forced the ship to put into the harbor at Takao until the storm abated. Along with the heavy winds and ominous clouds, the temperature dropped significantly. It was no longer suffocatingly hot in the hold, but the change was no improvement. All of us had by then spent well over a year in the tropics. Our blood was thin and the few clothes we had left were lightweight. Those factors, coupled with the sickness and malnutrition we had experienced, left us unable to cope with the cold. As though by design, the Japanese finally rigged a wind-scoop that brought air sweeping into the hold, and the cold came down the hatchway as well as through the thin hull. There was no escape from it. In addition to our other miseries, there was a bad scare on our way into the harbor, a submarine alert accompanied by shouting and scurrying about on the deck. A torpedo from an American submarine prowling in the area actually did cross our bow, but did not hit or detonate. Some of the later ships were not so fortunate; for example, the *Oryoko Maru* was bombed by our own Air Corps off Subic Bay, with the loss of over four hundred prisoner lives. It too was not identifiable as a carrier of prisoners. The survivors were put aboard another ship which was also sunk, this time in the vicinity of Formosa. Only a few hundred survived the second sinking. Other ships met a similar fate. There were only eighty-two survivors of the original fifteen hundred aboard the *Arisan Maru,* which was torpedoed in the China Sea late in 1944. The small number remaining from the more than three thousand who started out on those two ships had two things in common, quiet heroism and an endurance beyond what we think of as the limits of human capacity. By comparison, the horrors of the Death March and Camp O'Donnell had been merely warming-up exercises.

The cold probably saved my life and certainly saved my sanity. We could hear the propeller shaft turning under us all the time, and I asked Jim how the crew made their inspections and did the necessary lubrication. He told me the shaft was in a steel tunnel and that the engineering people had access to that tunnel through the engine room bulkhead. This information gave me an idea; why not attempt to get into that warm room? Jim agreed with me. There were probably other openings into the tunnel in addition to the one from the engine room, and we decided to look for one of them, hoping that we could get inside that shell and thence into the engine room where we could get out of the cold. We found an access door near the stern and were able to open it. Once inside the narrow passageway, it was a simple matter to follow it back to the engine room, and the transit was an eerie experience. Where we entered we could hear clearly the churning of the propeller in the sea, with the slide of water past the hull as a hissing accompaniment. These sounds gradually faded as we worked our way forward and they were replaced by the low hum of the shaft turning in its bearings. We had no light, so had to grope our way very carefully to avoid being trapped by the rotation of the shaft or caught by the bolts that held its sections together. We finally reached the bulkhead safely. It took a while to muster sufficient courage to open the hatch, because we knew that if caught we could expect immediate punishment, even death. The possible benefits outweighed the risk, and we inched the door open a little at a time until we could see the entire compartment. There was nobody there, but there was light. Thank God it was warm, and we entered, leaving the hatch open for a quick getaway if necessary. Both of us were light-headed with a combination of tension, fear and hope. It took a while to settle down and take stock of the situation, and even longer to realize our good fortune.

That engine room became our home for the next few days, and I'll try to describe it. The engine itself was a single steam cylinder mounted vertically in the center of the compartment. The piston rod turned a crank that was attached to the propeller shaft, and both of them were protected by the open cast iron framework that also served as the supporting base for the cylinder. The insulated pipes that carried both supply and exhaust steam between the engine and the boiler in another compartment were close overhead. An oil reservoir tank near the machine, with lines running to the slides, the end bearings on the piston rod and other moving parts, provided lubrication for them. With the exception of a few pressure and temperature gauges, there was little else in the room. It was a very simple arrangement which was probably operated from a central control panel in the boiler room, because we rarely saw anyone there. We could use a pile of oily rags for a bed, and best of all there was a tap, the water both fresh and cold. We would have to figure a way to get food, but were infinitely better off than we had been a few hours earlier. We even found egress to the deck without going back through the tunnel, and didn't worry too much about being caught. We had discovered a haven seldom visited by the crew, and there were places to hide when they did visit. The Japanese had never gone down into the POW hold, and if they had, the misery there was so great that our absence would not have been noticed by them. The prisoners would probably have welcomed it because that much space had been opened up for others. We did let Cory know about our good luck, and he shared the compartment with us for a short time, but we told nobody else. Our sanctuary was too small to accomodate more and to have spread the knowledge further would have been fatal. That seems to have been a most self-centered action, but at that point personal survival was the over-riding concern for each of us, and anything which jeopardized it was unthinkable. We had found that haven. We had taken the risk. We alone would take refuge there.

After five days in Takao, the storm abated enough for the ship to proceed toward Japan. Several days later we dropped anchor in the port of Shimonoseki. During that time more died and were buried at sea. Our guard force began to realize the frightful conditions in the hold, probably because of the death toll, and made some attempt to improve them by allowing more prisoners on deck at a time and for longer periods. They also lowered high-pressure hoses into the hold and washed it down with sea water, pumping the muck over the side with the bilge pumps. That improved things a little for a couple of days, but neither the food nor the drinking water supply was increased. There were no medicines to be had, so conditions quickly reverted to what they had been before the clean-up. It was a miserable group that took its first look at Japan on Thanksgiving Day of 1942, without any of the optimism that had been so strong when we left Cabanatuan.

14

Steelworker

The last Thursday of November in 1942 was cold and bleak, with low cloud cover and a hint of moisture in the air. It fit both our mood and our prospects for the future, given our experience on the XX Maru. We remained aboard the ship in the port of Shimonoseki while the Japanese troops were disembarked into lighters and ferried to shore. Our turn came next and it was a long process, since so many required assistance and only a hundred or so could be taken at a time. I was in one of the first groups, and we were forced to stand on the dock in the raw wind until the balance of the approximately fourteen hundred men remaining after that harrowing voyage could join us on the pier. We made a sorry spectacle for the curious crowd of civilians that soon gathered, dressed as we were in the remnants of tropical uniforms, thin, emaciated and filthy from those weeks in that awful hold. Unlike the crowds we had last seen in Manila, these people exhibited no evidence of encouragement or support. The message they sent was mildly contemptuous since they could not understand why we were prisoners at all, considering their *samurai* background.

After assembly was complete, we were formed into a rough column four abreast for the march from the pier to the railroad station a short distance away. There we were divided into groups of about four hundred men each, and dispatched by train to the widely separated locations where we would spend the next increment of our captivity. Shimonoseki lies at the western tip of the island of Honshu, the largest of the Japanese chain, directly across a narrow strait separating that island from Kyushu. Our route was northeasterly, and took us through Hiroshima, Okayama and Kobe on the way into Osaka. We didn't get to see much of the countryside because the blackout curtains in all the cars were drawn tight, and guards patrolled the aisles to prevent "spying." However, as we neared journey's end, there were a few opportunities for quick looks at both Kobe and Osaka, which appear separated on the map, but are actually contiguous. There were miles of wooden houses interspersed here and there with taller office buildings and factories. The streets were teeming with people who were walking and bicycling, but very few were in cars or trucks. It reminded me of sprawling and busy Los Angeles.

There were forty-six officers and three hundred fifty-four enlisted men in our group. We found we were destined to be laborers in a steel factory on the outskirts of Osaka. Our services would be contracted to the operators by the Army, and we would be used wherever work was needed. This arrangement was another violation of the Geneva Convention, which prohibits the use of prisoners of war in an industry supporting the military in any way. But we were in no position to argue, having learned long since about its futility and the reprisals that inevitably followed such attempts. We were indifferent and so happy to get off that bloody ship that nothing else mattered.

I began to get an idea on our ride from the railroad station to the camp just how much the Japanese people were sacrificing in order to support their war effort. The vehicles we rode in were powered by gasoline engines which had been converted to burn coal gas or acetylene, either fuel generated in small pots attached to the running-board of each truck. They were old and inefficient, and we made frequent stops for adjustments and minor repairs. Even this early in the war there were some food shortages, and ragged clothing was the rule rather than the exception. Few of the people we passed along the way seemed happy, even though their armies were still dominant in most parts of the Pacific. In a way it gave me some degree of hope for the future, because I could contrast what I was seeing with my memories of the abundance in the United States. I thought to myself that sooner or later the difference in resources available would be felt and that the U. S. would emerge as the ultimate victor. My resolve to be patient, and concentrate on the present without too much concern for the long term, was reinforced by the impressions of that day. I was more than ever determined to see it through to the end if that were physically possible.

Thus, I was not too discouraged when we arrived at the steel factory in the afternoon, despite the very unprepossessing appearance of that collection of rusty sheet metal buildings. The *Yodogawa Seiko* (Yodogawa Steel Company) was located on the banks of the Yodo River (in Japanese, *Yodogawa*), and took its name from that. It was characterized by the usual slag pile, the smoke and dust, the crushed cinders in the yard and rust everywhere there was metal. Partitions had been installed to isolate a corner of one of the steel buildings that we would use as a temporary barracks, and sleeping platforms covered with thin *tatami* (woven straw mats) had been built. There was a fifty gallon drum in the center which served as a charcoal-burning stove, the sole source of heat in that large room. Smoke and dust from the factory operations on the other side of the partitions were in the air, but the thing that caught my eye was a stack of five blankets placed at each sleeping spot. I hadn't had a blanket for months and had worried how to survive the cold winter ahead with nothing but tropical rags, so this was a very welcome sight. The guards placed one of us in front of each sleeping spot, where we were required to stand at attention while the camp commander, an Army lieutenant, delivered a speech through an interpreter. It was less bombastic than those we had heard in the past but no less emphatic about what would be expected of us. Each man would be issued a name tag with a number on it. There would be a morning roll call *(tenko)* every day and each man would have to shout his Japanese number in order, until all were accounted present. This routine would be followed by breakfast, after which work details would be formed and marched to their respective working places throughout the plant. There would be a short rest period in the middle of the day and a small lunch, then details would be formed again for the afternoon's work. At the end of the shift we would be marched back to the open area by the barracks, counted, and searched to assure that nothing had been stolen during the day. After this there would be the evening meal, and then we could have some free time before the lights were turned off for the night. The routine would not vary except for an occasional day off. For this night only, the Japanese had provided the evening meal, but beginning the next morning our own cooks would prepare all the food. The senior officer in our group would act as prisoner camp commander and be the liaison between the Japanese staff and ourselves. There would be no fraternization between the Japanese workers and the prisoners. Other restrictions were imposed, but by that time no one paid much attention, because we had heard most of it before several times. By the end of his speech it was dark and we were ready to hit the sack, even without a meal.

Then came a complete surprise. He told us that nobody could eat or do anything else except practice *tenko* until each of us had had a bath. We had not seen any evidence yet of facilities for that and it was the first time in our odyssey that any of our captors had even suggested such a thing. After nineteen days on the XX *Maru* the prospect of a bath, any bath, was like going to Valhalla.

All had been assigned a sleeping place, the officers grouped together, and each person was assigned a number. Mine was 360, in *Nippon-go* (Japanese language) *san hyaku roku-ju*, a tongue-twister that for the purposes of the *tenko* became "sambyaku rokuju" shouted at the top of the voice as rapidly as possible. We had a couple of practice counts before the bath details were formed and I suppose the results were amusing, because all the guards snickered, but we finally completed one to their satisfaction. There were a few more instructions, but the prospect of a bath was too pre-eminent in our minds for them to be absorbed. And finally it came. We were divided into groups of twenty or thirty and ordered to disrobe—not a problem since we weren't wearing much. One group at a time was ushered out of the barracks area, across the building floor and into a closed-in section from which we could see steam escaping. Its floor was tiled and there were small wooden buckets scattered about the edges. In the center was what looked like a shallow rectangular swimming pool, with steam rising from it into the cool air. There were two or three Japanese already in the pool who politely paid no attention to us at all. The interpreter demonstrated the bath protocol. First, we were to stand at the edge of the pool and scoop water out of it with wooden buckets, using that for a thorough washing of body and hair. Other bucketfuls would be needed to rinse away the soap and dirt into the gutter at the outer edge of the room. Because we were so dirty, the process would be repeated until we were clean enough to get into the pool. Apparently, the pool was to be used for soaking only. The water was hot and the strong soap was plentiful. Finally I became really clean for the first time in months, and the sensation was heavenly. Immersion, though, seemed closer to hell than heaven, because the water in the bath was hotter than anything I had ever experienced. I inched myself in a fraction at a time until fully immersed except for my head, and soaked for a while. It never was totally comfortable, but became bearable, and I could feel the tension and strain draining away. While I was trying to adjust to the heat, those Japanese already in the bath got out, toweled themselves vigorously and left, and I realized that two of them were women. In our condition, no one raised an eyebrow. The women were completely unself-conscious about nudity, and the other natives paid no attention. I still had a lot to learn.

When the bath was over, we shivered back to the barracks, dressed, had a small bowl of rice and then went to bed for the first comfortable night's sleep in many months. I folded my blankets into a sleeping bag, some under as well as over me, laid my head on the small, round rice-husk pillow furnished with the other bedding and fell asleep immediately. ''Fell'' is an appropriate word: it was just like dropping into a well, and happened about as fast. But morning brought back the reality of our situation. We were wakened early by the stomping of the guards in their hob-nailed shoes. They aligned us in front of the sleeping bays, in the same order as on the previous night, at attention on the command of *Kiotsuke*, shouted as ''. . . tskay!,'' with the accent on the last syllable. Next came *Bango!* (count off), and all four hundred of us, one by one, had to yell his number for the roll call. Some had forgotten theirs and for a little while there was confusion, but rifle butts and kendo sticks helped to resolve it quickly, and tenko proceeded to its conclusion. At the end another command, *Yasume!*, allowed us to stand at ease though still in formation. We were treated to another speech outlining still more rules: wake at six o'clock, dress, stack the blankets neatly, clean up the sleeping area and be ready for *tenko* at six-ten. All this was the responsibility of Major William Reardon, the senior American and the prisoner camp commander. The guards would take roll call and after that no one was to recline on his bunk until the evening meal was finished. *Tenko* over, we would be allowed to clean up at the washrack located in a separate outbuilding, and must be ready for breakfast by six-thirty. Work details would form at seven and the day's labor would begin. The prisoner cooks were selected, one officer in charge with about six enlisted men. Lt. Ollie Lancaster, a would-be politician from Tallahassee, Florida drew this duty. He along with his helpers were thus assured that they, at least, would not go hungry. Cooks never did.

The kitchen was in a small building just outside the door of the barracks, and Ollie and his crew were learning its intricacies and preparing breakfast under the eyes of a guard. The rest of us, in the meantime, were required to fill out forms giving essential personal information: name, rank, serial number, home address and social class. The latter was a puzzler because we don't have such a rigid social structure in the States, and I can't explain their reason for wanting the information. The form had three boxes labeled "Upper," "Middle" and "Lower." Over the years following we had to fill out several of these, and I always checked "Upper," knowing our feudal hosts were very class conscious. I hoped that my small deception might accrue some advantage. It never did, but seemed worth a try. A breakfast consisting of rice and thin green soup was finally delivered in wooden pails. It was ladled into our mess-kits, quan cans or other personal containers, under the watchful eyes of both the guards and the prisoners. Close monitoring of the servers had become habit, a means of assuring that the distribution was fair and nobody got a grain more than his share. We ate in silence, each wondering about the work we would be forced to do and worrying whether we were up to it. Immediately after the meal, details of about twenty men including at least one officer were formed, who were supposed to work together for the balance of our stay in Yodogawa.

Today we are told all about the efficiency of Japanese steel-making. That old plant was much different; its equipment came right out of the dark ages and the process depended heavily on human effort. The factory made steel castings for many purposes, from small items like scissor blades and hand pliers to large casings for high pressure steam turbines. A large proportion of its output was engine blocks and cylinder heads for the diesel motors which the Japanese used for propulsion on the barges that plied the coastal rivers and canals. There were several metal-clad buildings in the complex, used for various purposes: storage of supplies and materials, making sand molds into which molten metal was cast, casting the desired shapes and making steel. Hematite (iron ore), coke, limestone and scrap metal were stacked in large open piles, and the traffic areas were covered with packed cinders from the furnaces. The whole plant was dusty, rusty and smoky.

The details marched out of the building to our work stations. My group was assigned to one of the two blast furnaces. Our function was to feed raw materials, draw the slag (waste) at intervals, tap the product into shallow trenches, forming the bars called "pigs," and then to break up the pigs into short pieces after they cooled. The blast furnace was a vertical cylinder thirty or forty feet tall and ten feet in diameter. Raw materials were hand-fed through a feed port a little over twenty feet above ground level and finished steel was drawn out at the bottom. The slag port was six or seven feet up, and oxygen required for the process was supplied through a leaky network of pipes coming from a compressor. The molten steel, when tapped, flowed from the lower draw-port through a series of ditches into shallow trenches dug in the sand, where it was allowed to cool and harden. There was a long stairway leading from the ground to the feed port, where all raw materials were introduced into the melting chamber. Scrap metal was carried up the long stairway piece by piece. The other ingredients, hematite, limestone and coke, were carried in shallow woven bamboo baskets suspended by a wire harness from a wooden pole.

We found that the work was demanding and arduous. Prisoners took part in all the steel-making steps, but at a much slower pace than the Japanese. It was exhausting, because unused and wasted muscles were simply not capable of sustained effort. For example, two men were required to carry the baskets up the stairway, one at each end of the pole. The Japanese workers thought this was hilarious; one of them could carry two baskets at a time by himself. But they were well-fed and strong, and had been doing this job for years. Curiously, those years of doing the same thing had developed thick muscle pads on their carrying shoulders, something like calluses, which easily identified them for what they were, beasts of burden. Handling the pigs was the hardest. Part of our work party had to break them loose from the feed sprues with sledge hammers and carry them, using special tongs, to a storage pile. It was back-breaking work, literally, and cost me corrective surgery on my own spine after the war was over.

We also broke up the pigs from the blast furnaces, again using sledge hammers, and inserted them into a separate casting furnace where they were re-melted. The "melt" was carried to previously prepared sand molds in large vessels by overhead crane, and carefully poured into the mold through a sprue. Other prisoner crews took part in all these steps exept the preparation of the molds, which was deemed too technical for them, and also offered too many opportunities for sabotage. This paranoid fear on their part was laughable, because no sabotage was needed. More than sixty percent of the plant output was rejected routinely by the inspectors because of blowholes, thin spots, poor grain size or some other defect. However, that did not allay the suspicion of the Japanese toward us, which was to become an unwarranted cause for many serious and brutal confrontations in the ensuing months. All we did was hard physical labor, made even more so by our debilitated condition. It was complicated by the almost total lack of effective communication between us, the guards and the regular factory workers. Misunderstandings were inevitable, and they caused much re-work, wasted effort and more brutality. None of us had the strength or the energy for that.

The factory operators were responsible for the care and feeding of the prisoners, and the Osaka district of the Army for administration of the camp. Each man's food ration, at the outset, amounted to six hundred grams of unpolished rice per day, of fair quality. In addition we had a small supply of vegetables for soups, consisting of a few beans, large pickled white radishes called *daikon,* greens of some kind, and limited quantities of salt, sugar and other staples. This was the nominal ration; in practice it was smaller, because the soldiers appropriated many items for their own use, particularly the beans, sugar and salt. We had to subsist on very much less than an adequate diet for inactive people, even worse for those expected to perform hard labor.

After a few weeks, we began to feel the results, in the onset of dietary deficiency diseases beyond those we had brought with us from the Philippines. The consequence was to be expected, a death rate that climbed steadily through the winter, and an increasing number of men unable to report for work because of illness. We already had experience with scurvy and pellagra, but worse than those was beri-beri, which affects the nervous system particularly in the lower extremities. There were two varieties of this disease, which we called "wet" and "dry." Wet beri-beri is swelling from edema, caused by the inability of the body to throw off liquids. The hands and arms are affected, but swelling of the legs and groin was the most no-

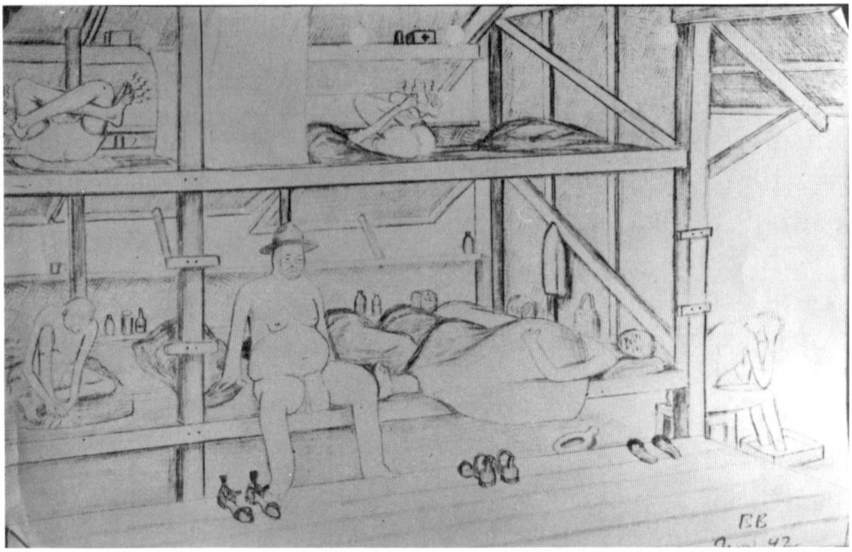

Beri-beri Sufferers

ticeable and caused many problems. It was extremely painful and greatly restricted movement. The sight of scrotums grown to the size of softballs is not pretty. The most serious of the two types was dry beri-beri, because it was excruciatingly painful and left permanent damage. My layman's understanding is that it causes deterioration of the sheath surrounding the nerves, leaving them exposed to trauma and pressure, and results in agony at the slightest touch. The deterioration is progressive, and reaches a point where blood circulation is impaired and even stopped. The ultimate result is tissue degeneration and death, and many toes were amputated by the prisoner doctor to prevent the spread of gangrene. This operation was accomplished without the benefit of anesthetic; the nerves were dead by then and the pain was gone. All of us were afflicted to one degree or another by beri-beri, and those who still survive will carry some adverse symptoms of it to their graves.

At first, there was no doctor among the prisoner group, and what treatment there was came from Japanese medical corpsmen who were untrained and uninterested in improving conditions. There were few very effective medicines, which consisted of weak pain-killers and powders supposedly containing the vitamins we lacked. These were doled out grudgingly, and there was never enough to do much good. Consequently, the line at sick call grew with each day, and conditions became so bad that we were finally able to convince *Yamada Shoi* we needed a medical doctor to take care of the inevitable industrial injuries that occurred in the plant, as well as the illnesses that plagued us. Doctor Richardson was transferred from one of the other camps, and I believe the Japanese were secretly glad to be relieved of a responsibility they could not handle. However, the corpsmen were still there and had the power to over-ride the decisions of our doctor if they chose, which happened often. I was reminded again of those poor doctors at O'Donnell, who had to stand by and watch their patients wither away without being able to help. On rare occasions, a medical examiner from the military came to Yodogawa *Bunsho* (sub-camp) ostensibly to assure we were being cared for properly. Those visits were always hurried and the examinations were perfunctory, performed without genuine interest or follow-up.

Apparently, the factory owners felt they were not getting their money's worth from POW work, and the general ration was cut in mid-December to five hundred seventy grams of rice per person, beans were eliminated and sugar and salt grossly reduced. If that were not enough, the rations were halved for those who were unable to report for work, making it nearly impossible for the sick to recover. As it had been in O'Donnell, the sick bay became a place to be avoided at all costs, given the near certainty that those who entered it would leave in a four foot square wooden box. After a death, the box would be delivered to the sick bay, the naked body would be stuffed in and the box carted off to a crematory. In due course a six inch square, white cardboard box, marked with *Kanji* characters identifying the ashes, would be returned to us. By the time I left Yodogawa in June there were more than eighty of those, macabre reminders of the futility of our existence.

In addition to my factory job, I worked part time with the invalids in sick bay. That included frequent changes of bedding to clean up the excrement and kill the lice and bedbugs. We kept a fire going in the yard outside the kitchen under a fifty-gallon drum, where we boiled contaminated blankets and clothing to get rid of the filth and the pests, but it gave only temporary respite. Almost as soon as the blankets were put back into service, they became reinfested and the process would have to start all over. It was a gut-wrenching experience when cleaning up after a death, to be watched by ten or fifteen pairs of glazed eyes and have someone say, "Lieutenant, you can do that for me tomorrow." I knew that it would happen. Most often the illness would be real, but sometimes it was just a case of giving up; the will to live had been lost. There was nothing more I could say or do to help, and I have lived with the frustration of that failure ever since, to my ever-lasting sorrow. There I learned another survival skill: the control of depression, perhaps more insidious and lethal than the diseases with which we were now so familiar. Everyone was affected by it to some degree and it took a conscious and continuous effort to overcome. Never allow the overwhelming daily stress to obscure the ultimate goal. Immerse ones' self in helping others where possible, realizing that in so doing personal psychological problems are minimized to the point that they are bearable. Search always for the bright side of any situation, even though its light may be very dim most of the time. This approach, partly deliberate and partly instinctive, was vital to the preservation of mental and physical stability. I could sense it in myself and observe it working for others, who almost always were the ones contributing to the general welfare of the camp.

The acquisition of medicine and food was not the only problem we faced. Clothing and the bedding that might keep out the winter's cold were of great concern for the months of December, January, February and March that still lay ahead. We found that the blankets that had looked so enticing on our first night in *Yodogawa Bunsho* were illusory, like most of the largess provided by the Japanese. They were shoddy, thin and incapable of retaining the heat needed to offset the cold of those long winter nights. Until about the tenth of December, we had to make do with the clothing we had brought with us, which was suited only for tropical climates. Near that date, we were forced to turn in all those items,and they were replaced by Japanese clothing. We now wore cotton underpants tied in place at the waist with a string and a thin undershirt, collarless and buttoned up the front. The trousers they issued were a loosely woven dark green material with little body, but very good ventilation, and the jackets were the same type, buttoned up the front like the undershirts and providing little warmth. Socks were multi-layer items called *tabi*, which fastened at the rear of the foot by hooks and separated the big toe from the rest. They were used by the Japanese to match with *geta* (wooden clogs) which are much like the sandals seen on many of our beaches today. The clog had two cleats on the bottom, front and rear, to keep the foot out of the mud during wet weather. Sometimes it worked, but the combination of *tabi* and *geta* was never comfortable for me. To complete the ensemble, there was a threadbare Japanese army coat, used and then discarded long ago by the original owners as unsuited to ward off the damp cold of a Japanese winter. The entire ensemble was not much more effective than the clothing we had been wearing, but looked better because it was uniform. Incidentally, the racket made by those wooden sandals on the wooden floor of our barracks was overwhelming. Our hosts solved that problem by forcing their removal at the top of the stairs leading to the sleeping area. They had to be hand-carried to our bunks, set precisely at the foot and left there until it was time to depart for the next day's work.

By this time, we had moved from temporary quarters to another barracks that was not much better. It was a second floor built into an open steel-sheeted warehouse, accessible by one set of stairs leading up from the guardpost and another, which was locked most of the time, used on infrequent trips to the bath-house. The building was uninsulated and the only source of heat was another of those fifty gallon drum stoves, burning charcoal. The warmth was great for those within ten feet of the barrel, but not even noticeable at the ends of the room. Even our captors noticed the effects of the cold on us and finally issued different clothing, consisting of worn army uniforms, khaki, bi-layered and close woven, which looked and felt like canvas. They were much warmer than the green stuff and we didn't complain.

The unvarying routine of our day was to assemble in the yard just outside the guardpost between the kitchen and the washrack, form the details and march off to the workplace. At the end of the day the various groups would re-assemble in the same spot for count and inspection before being dismissed. If there had been some infraction of the rules the formation was held at rigid attention for up to an hour, despite fatigue or other problems. Not all Japanese were without compassion and occasionally there would be some contraband: a bit of food, some dried fish or a few cigarettes. It might have been a gift or traded for something of value. Its discovery caused all kinds of repercussions as well as severe punishment for the offender. Sometimes he alone would be singled out, but frequently the whole group was punished. One such incident was typical. About the end of December, 1942, we were issued brand new US Army shoes through the International Red Cross. It was a great event and the first indication we had that the outside world was even aware of our existence. The fly in the ointment was that we were not allowed to wear them. They were to be stored on the shelf above our sleeping space and kept shined and laced for the benefit of army inspectors on their periodic visits. About two weeks later, one pair was missing, and the camp was turned upside down to find them. They were located in the possession of one of the factory workers , who had traded a box of dried fish to one of our men for the shoes. That worker was summarily executed. The guilty prisoner was not, but might as well have been. He was stripped naked and forced to kneel on the sharp cinders of the yard for a full day. He could not relax at all because of a sharp-sided stick tied behind his knees, which prevented any attempt to sit back on his haunches, and his hands were tied behind him. We were required to watch him for several hours before being allowed in the barracks, and we listened to his cries all through the night and into the next day. The trauma and the exposure were too much for him, and he died two days later. The Japanese man had been lucky.

The daily inspections served another purpose, to identify the slackers. Everyone was required to extend his hands, palm up, while the guards went down the line feeling each pair. They were looking for calluses. If you had them you were a good worker. If not, you weren't doing your job and were subjected to verbal and physical punishment in addition to a possible cut in rations. The system was a very simple and direct form of what we now call personnel motivation.

In addition to the shoes the Red Cross had sent enough food parcels to provide one for each prisoner. However, they were issued to us on the basis of one parcel for each three men. Even so, it was a wonderful bonus, as it contained the first solid food we had eaten since the horses in Bataan. In each box was a can of corned beef, a can of Spam, dried milk, chocolate bars, canned cheese and butter, soap and seven packs of American cigarettes. This was paradise indeed, especially for the smokers; the non-smokers traded their cigarettes for food at very high prices. Those parcels, about fourteen inches square and six inches deep, were a tremendous boost to morale, even when divided among three people. They had a better effect than a week off from the blast furnace. There would be others later, but none would have the impact of that first one. I, for one, have been a strong supporter of the Red Cross ever since. I feel that we probably owe our survival to the supplemental food they furnished us over the following few years.

There was comedy in addition to the tragedy. One evening I was called into the prisoner office by Yamada Shoi (2nd Lieutenant Yamada), the camp commander. He had brought with him a small bottle of sake and a package of Sakura cigarettes, Japan's best. He ceremoniously poured a cup of the sake and lighted one of the cigarettes for me, then proceeded to give me some bad news. He had read that Salt Lake City had been shelled by a Japanese submarine and had suffered heavy damage. His records showed that I lived in Salt Lake, and he had probably noticed me around the camp, so decided I should know about the incident. Yamada had no information as to casualties, but hoped that my family was not among them. The sake and cigarettes were his way of expressing sympathy and condolence. The news did not bother me very much, since my home town was more than seven hundred miles from the coast and could not possibly have been touched by any artillery fire of that day. However, I understood enough by then of Oriental "face" to know that informing him of his error would cause him acute embarrassment. I carefully concealed from him my amusement at his appalling ignorance of geography and accepted his concern at face value. Further reflection tempered my amusement because I suddenly realized that my ignorance of Japanese geography was as great as his was about America. I didn't have even the vaguest idea where Kyoto was located, for example. We finished off the sake and he presented me with the remainder of the package of cigarettes. Yamada spoke some English and we were able to talk a little about the war. He had been a school-teacher and wanted to return to that field, so army service was an interlude to be endured, but not enjoyed. We didn't discuss the causes of the war, which neither of us understood anyway, but we did agree it should end soon. In a way, I treasure that brief encounter because it put the conflict into perspective from both sides, and reminded me that both of us were individuals caught up in a situation we could not control or affect in any material way.

This encounter with Yamada Shoi led to a change in assignment for me that made life much easier. A couple of days later he came into the office and presented me with a small, red English-Japanese dictionary. His orders were that I should study it and learn how to communicate directly with the foremen and workers in the plant. The hope was that in so doing I could alleviate some of the difficulties caused by poor communication between the factory workers and the prisoners of war. I took on the assignment with enthusiasm as a way to avoid more debilitating physical labor. The study was easier than I had anticipated and gave me a chance to exercise my mind. Conversational, street level Japanese is relatively simple to learn, and there was no reason for me to study more sophisticated forms. There was no reason to study the written language either, because that would have taken years, and I didn't have time for that. *Kanji* consists of about fifty-five thousand ideographs, and in addition to being the written word is an art form, a skill highly regarded in Japan. My simple objective was to be able to converse with the factory worker and the private soldier in terms all of us could understand, about the kinds of problems we faced daily. I never became an expert, and there was as much communication with smiles, bows and gestures as there was with words. But we were able to avoid some of the conflicts that had caused so much trouble in our first months, so the effort was worthwhile. I still have the dictionary.

Yamada *Shoi* was replaced as camp commander by his assistant, Hirose *Gunso* (Sergeant Hirose), in February of 1943. Hirose was more harsh and less fair than Yamada and somewhat quixotic, and occasionally did things for the prisoners that were beyond our normal expectations. For example, in one of his daily reports, Dr. Richardson noted that many of us had badly deteriorating teeth. The sergeant decided that he would take a group of the worst cases to the *ha ishia* (dentist). About a week later, a dozen of us, escorted by Hirose and a guard, marched into Osaka for treatment. I would rather have stayed home. The dentist's office was shabby and not too clean, and its equipment must have been manufactured some time before the turn of the century. The chair was worn out, its upholstery torn, with horsehair extruding from holes and cracks. Sanitation devices consisted of a grimy glass and a spittoon. Worse than these was the drill. It was powered by a foot treadle like those on old Singer sewing machines, giving motion to the drill-head through a knotted cord running over a flywheel and a series of small pulleys. The *ha ishia* stood over the patient, one foot on the floor and the other pumping away on the treadle more or less steadily while he worked on a cavity. He was quite a contortionist and it was his only talent. He certainly had not been trained by Painless Parker, had the chairside manner of a pit bull and would have laughed at the thought of using anesthesia. He pulled two of my teeth and gouged holes in three others. The other patients had a similar happy experience, and all of us agreed to be very busy if anyone even hinted at a return engagement. Hirose re-returned us to the bunsho, very proud of his humanitarian accomplishment. We could have killed him.

Sergeant Hirose was infinitely better than his successor, Nakajima *Gunso,* who was a bastard. He was a provincial, uneducated peasant who knew nothing and could care less about anything outside his own particular sphere, and was, like Col. Tsuji, a fanatic. He was slender and his manner was waspish. His enforcment of camp rules was harsh and his understanding of our situation minimal. The natural result of his methods was a sharp decline in productivity and a rapid increase in those confined to sick bay. The worse conditions became, the more violent were his reactions, and the spring and early summer were a nightmare. We kept records, and by the first of June, 1943, 21 percent of the original four hundred had perished. Others had been sent to ''hospitals'' and we never heard whether they lived or died. Nakajima seemed to blame this attrition on us and his behavior became even more irrational. He even accused me of being a spy, since I was by then able to speak a little *Nippon-go,* and ordered me to stop using that acquired skill immediately.

I had other problems besides being a spy; the most painful of them pellagra. It is a deficiency disease similar to scurvy, in which the inner surfaces of the mouth become afflicted by painful open lesions, which get progressively worse. The sores even caused pain when I tried to take a drink of water. Again, no remedy was available until one of the cooks, a dark young fellow from New Mexico, befriended me. He approached me one day and said, ''Lieutenant, I can cure that for you if you will eat what I fix.'' So far as I could see there wasn't much he could do, but I gave him my mess-kit and awaited the outcome. The next day he brought it back, steamy hot and speckled with all the varieties of pepper he had been able to obtain. He told me to eat it and then he would bring another; after that I wouldn't need any more. The first bite convinced me. There wouldn't be any other bites. Nothing could have hurt so much, even childbirth. I felt as though I had been cauterized and would have given up the whole idea except that he stood over me and cajoled me into finishing that fiery concoction. It took a day and a half and then he fixed up another of the same, only marginally easier to ingest than the first. Two or three days later the symptoms began to disappear, and in another week I was cured. Dr. Richardson was as mystified as I, but one thing is sure, Mexican food has been high on my preference list ever since. Pepper must be loaded with vitamins.

By the middle of June we had had our fill of Nakajima Gunso, and so were not at all disappointed when informed that twenty-five of the remaining officers were to be transferred away from Yodogawa Bunsho to another camp. We didn't know where it would be or what it would be like, but the optimism that had flared and died so many times in the past fourteen months rose once more. This time it would be warranted, though accompanying it would once again be the wrench of leaving behind friends made and tested in the cauldron of the past months. Among those were Major Reardon and Dr. Richardson. Jack Draper and John Davis, from Salt Lake, were included, as were Harry Menozzi and Frank Pasquale, both New Yorkers. Ollie Lancaster remained to run the kitchen, in which the Mexican friend who had cured my pellagra still worked.

Yodogawa Bunsho lasted as a work center until the American bombings in the spring of 1945 burned it out. At that time the ones left alive were transferred to another camp, where they remained until the end of the war.

15

Gentleman Farmer

For the first time in my captivity, luck was with me. The new camp to which our twenty-five man group was sent was Zentsuji, located on the island of Shikoku. Shikoku is a fairly large body of land lying in the obtuse angle formed by the larger islands of Honshu and Kyushu. Mostly agricultural, it was also used by the Japanese Army as a base for training their infantry troops prior to shipment overseas. In addition, there were many Buddhist and Shinto shrines, where people from all over the country made periodic pilgrimages to renew their faith and pray for the soldiers who were away. Zentsuji lay just across the fence from one of these shrines and we could hear many of the ceremonies that took place. One of the most interesting was the mass funeral for large groups of soldiers prior to their being sent to combat overseas. Each time a contingent finished its training there would be funeral service at the shrine with much pomp: cymbals clashing, music and vocal exhortations. The idea was that the individual would either come home victorious or die gloriously for the emperor. In the latter case, he would already have been assured entry into their heaven. To allow himself to be captured would have made him a non-person in the eyes of his countrymen. He was then considered dead and would be totally ignored by his family and townspeople alike thereafter. Understanding this did much to explain to us the attitude of the Japanese toward their own captives. It did not excuse their actions against us, but did clarify part of their reasoning.

The camp was two old army barracks enclosed by a high board fence. Auxiliary structures consisted of an enclosed latrine, an open washrack, the camp kitchen and a bath house with showers only. The barracks were long, two stories high, and contained sufficient room to accommodate seven hundred and fifty prisoners of war, the Japanese guard force and the administrative staff. Collected there were flotsam from campaigns all over the Pacific: Wake Island, Indonesia, Singapore, Rabaul, the Philippines and China. The majority were Americans, but there were also British, Australians and Dutch. Most were officers, though there were nearly a hundred enlisted men and even some civilian construction workers who had been taken on Wake Island very early in the war. Best of all, it was not a work camp: there were no blast furnaces to feed, no mines to dig and no dams to build. There was a small working party of enlisted men dispatched to the dock every day, but they were well-treated and through them a number of extra items filtered into the compound, most notably newspapers. Food was always short, but there was more of it and the quality was better than we had been furnished at Yodogawa. Everyone there was thin, but there was much less mental and physical illness, and the general attitude was infinitely better than anything we had experienced. The most telling difference was that, during the twenty-one months I was there, not a single death occurred, though there had been six or eight earlier, well before we arrived. This circumstance was truly remarkable to those of us who had watched more than half our number disappear between April of 1942 and June of 1943. The segregation of officers, better treatment and the absence of defense work were so unlike the Japanese that we found it difficult to understand. We finally concluded that this was a camp established for propaganda purposes, as a model demonstrating to the world that Nippon was as enlightened and humane as any other nation. We knew that wasn't true, but were more than willing to enjoy any benefits of their intended deception.

The men from Yodogawa were quartered in an open room at the top of the stairs, on the second floor of the east building. A central hallway extended the full length of the floor, with sleeping bays of equal size on both the north and south sides of it. Each bay had an open area in the center furnished with a table, and a sleeping platform against both walls. At the ends of the room were two large windows equipped with blackout curtains, which could be opened to provide cross-ventilation for the twin areas. A shelf for personal possessions ran the width of the bay above the platforms. The platforms were covered with the inevitable *tatami* and each could accommodate about seven men allowing an intimate but adequate twenty-two inches per person. As in Yodogawa, there were shoddy blankets and a rice-husk pillow, all kept neatly stacked at the head of the pad during the day. The platform was long enough for me, but some of the taller men had a little trouble with their feet hanging out over the edge at night. Our two bays were separated from the adjacent ones by partitions, forming an enclosure housing the twenty-eight people who would sleep and eat, work and take their recreation together for many months. We came to know each other: our outlooks on life, habits, strengths and weaknesses. We learned to know our room mates as well as most men get to know their wives over many years of marriage. It required a lot of tolerance and understanding to avoid conflict because everything a man did or said was known to all the others immediately. Even your thoughts seemed to be common property.

Everyone had his idiosyncracies. Paul Shure slept clear across the hall from me next to the north window. He must have had strong teeth, because he ground them together constantly during his sleep, and it was necessary to wake him frequently to stop the noise. Andy Anderson, a mining engineer commissioned during the war, loved to talk and could be counted on to keep it up all day. He would have talked all night too if we had not shut him down periodically. On one side of me was Fred Wildish, who seemed simple but wasn't, and had a low chuckle that made me feel good whenever I heard it. His best friend was tall, auburn-haired Jim Coffee who possessed a wry wit that could cut or heal with equal ease. Jim Baldwin, who had used the engine room on the *XX Maru* with me, was on my other side, and we were as compatible as ever. Next to him were the Powell boys, both pilots; though unrelated to each other they looked alike and formed a good team. Bob Silhavy and Gene Boyt shared almost everything together. They had been friends before the war and remain so even today. Bob was an inveterate, and expert, poker player. Kermit Lay was gregarious and interested in everyone. Norm Wides and Carroll Hines were buddies. Bearded Ralph Yoder was serious and could talk intelligently on any subject. Urban C. ''Hoppy'' Hoppman hardly talked at all. We got along well together and no one was an outcast. Life could have been pretty grim if it had been otherwise.

As I look back on the entire war from beginning to end, I have realized that one basic psychological need for everyone is some degree of personal privacy. This we did not have—ever. There was always someone watching our solitary walks around the camp perimeter; even in the *benjo* (toilet) we had company. Constant surveillance, whether it be by friend or enemy, is so wearing on the nerves that it is almost unbearable. Under normal conditions, all of us can get away for an hour or a day to be totally alone to idle, dream or otherwise renew ourselves, free from the pressures and demands of ordinary living. To be denied this luxury is to lose an essential element of living, and the loss of it for all those years left its imprint on each of us. Though I am now surrounded by a caring family and good friends, the requirement for solitude sometimes becomes irresistibly over-powering, and I retreat into my own private world for a while. I'm sure my family, especially my wife, has been puzzled by this, and without an understanding of my feelings, a little critical of my motivation. Perhaps this explanation, previously hazy in my own mind and articulated here for the first time, will help to ease their hurt and curiosity. I hope so.

The need for privacy notwithstanding, Zentsuji had other attributes which by our elemental standards were pleasant, especially when contrasted to the other camps. We had facilities for showering in a separate building near the *benjo*. In another gazebo-like structure was a long washrack fed by evenly spaced taps where we could wash in the morning and clean our clothing. The soap was strong but effective, and if you could stand a soapy cold water shave you could have one. Though many did some, like Yoder, chose to grow luxuriant beards instead, and that may have been wise. I used the same double-edged safety razor blade for the entire twenty-one months of my stay there. My beard is not tough, but with that dull blade I could feel the pull on each individual hair as it was hacked away. The blade could be "sharpened" by vigorous rubbing on the wetted inside surface of a round water glass. In retrospect, the difference before and after sharpening was probably imaginary, but I was able to keep that blade in service for a very long time.

There was room to exercise in the space between the buildings and the surrounding fence. When not on duty or otherwise occupied, we could walk to our hearts' content around the perimeter, approximately a quarter-mile per lap. I walked hundreds of them. Occasionally we were allowed to entertain ourselves with plays, skits and musicals written and staged by the prisoners. The British called them "concerts," and some of them were very good indeed, especially those performed at the Christmas season. The Aussies, the Brits and the Dutch all participated along with the Americans. There were no cliques and very little clannishness among the various groups. That aspect was much different from the initial atmosphere we had faced at both of the Cabanatuan camps, and infinitely more pleasant. We played a lot of bridge and poker, for money (yen), cigarettes or promissory notes. The stakes were unimportant; the objective was to pass the time.

Best of all, there were books to read, the first I had seen in nearly two years. Part of the library from the dismantled American embassy in Tokyo had found its way to Zentsuji and was available to us. I have always been a voracious reader, so for me that small library was a treasure trove and I kept a list of the titles read in a small schoolboys' notebook which I still have. There were a hundred and twenty-seven of them on that list: biography and autobiography, history, classical literature, historical and contemporary novels. I whiled away many peaceful hours reading some of those books several times. The Red Cross also sent a few books sometime in 1944. Their object must have been to provide some exercise to fallow minds because many were texts on such fascinating subjects as college algebra, calculus and business accounting. Most of those ended the war in almost new condition.

There were no newspapers allowed in the camp, and the possession of one was cause for harsh disciplinary action. Even so, the work detail that went out every day managed to smuggle about one a week into the compound. Of course, it was written in Japanese and undecipherable to all of us except a Navy lieutenant who had been assigned to the embassy as a language student before the war. He had learned to read the Kanji ideographs and the Katakana phonetic alphabet, and could translate. He would read the paper and then summarize its contents to a very small group. Those men, in turn, circulated through the camp and passed the news along to the rest of us, so that eventually everyone knew what was happening in the world. Almost all the news was propaganda, containing as it did reports of great victories by the Nipponese on land and sea. But even those reports were valuable, since it did not take very long to note that by this time their victories were being won in locations ever closer to the Japanese homeland. Nothing was said about losses. They loved to report the sinking of our largest aircraft carriers, one of which had been reported sent to the bottom at least four times over a period of several months. Even our guards noticed that odd fact, and one of them asked us how it was possible to raise and refit it so rapidly. He was told about our secret: certain large sections of the ship were filled with ping-pong balls, giving it the bouyancy to pop back to the surface by itself almost immediately. This seemed to satisfy him and he left happily. So the papers were a source of entertainment as well as news, and we looked forward to Lt. Jones' summaries with great anticipation. It took much courage for him to make them, and for the messengers to pass them along, because discussions of the war were verboten. Informed discussion would have triggered intensive investigation into the source of the news and severe reprisals against the offenders, including elimination of the dock details and beatings. Therefore we were very discreet about what was said, where and to whom. Hosetani was the official camp interpreter, a Japanese who had spent a good deal of time in the States. He fancied himselt a gum-shoe and loved to circulate through our area in an attempt to catch someone in a violation. Since there were so many of us, he always stood a good chance of being successful, and when he was, thoroughly enjoyed the repercussions. If he had discovered that we had our own carefully concealed interpreter, he would have had a field day.

Obviously, there was time for long conversations about almost anything. They covered a wide range of subjects with one notable exception: sex. This was surprising in a collection of mostly young men at the height of their virility, but our situation was unique. We were so preoccupied with food and survival and had been run-down for so long that fantasizing about sexual subjects had become very remote. I suspect that those who had been married before the war began were worried about their marriages and their own capacity to respond in the old ways. At any rate, sex was not a topic for discussion. Deliberate attempts to start such a diversion invariably foundered and the conversation switched to food and its preparation. Exotic menus were far more important than exotic mammaries.

All these advantages and distractions did not make Zentsuji a country club and we were always aware that we were prisoners. Each day started with the morning tenko, a parade-type formation held outside in all weather. This was followed by wash-up and breakfast, and then the work details were mustered and sent off for the day's labor. We had no war-related work to do, as they did in the other camps in Japan, but became farmers. Our job was to clear small plots of land in the vicinity, prepare the soil, plant some vegetable crop, then tend it until maturity and harvest. Our tools were primitive. We used old single blade mattocks and picks, a square-pointed spade, bentwood rakes and lots of muscle. The work days were about seven hours and we took our lunches with us: a handful of rice wrapped in a leaf. It was hard work and the results were poor. The small, hillside plots were dry and the soil was rocky. Water had to be carried in buckets and distributed, a dipper at a time, to each individual plant. We spent a lot of our time carrying stones from the field and piling them carefully around its edges, building fences similar to those seen in some sections of New England. We never harvested a crop because when our scraggly produce was ready, the Japanese would decide the land was needed for some other purpose and we were moved somewhere else. A new unimproved piece would be selected for cultivation and the whole process began again: clear, dig, carry rocks, turn the soil, plant and nurture, then leave. Everyone had to participate but those too old or sick or incapable for some other reason, and we accomplished a lot of rural beautification over those many months. But I don't remember ever eating a radish or a squash or any of the other crops so laboriously grown. Farming became a joke, done only because of the constant presence of alert armed guards who were very critical of shirkers and non-performers. We were slave labor without a purpose. There was one advantage. We got out in the sun and fresh air and away from the confining life of the barracks for four or five days a week. We fit the classic definition of the gentleman farmer; one who farms but never expects to make a profit from it.

Disciplinary surveillance was constant and rigid. Guards patrolled the fences and the interior areas constantly to prevent infractions of the rules. They did this at all hours of the day and night, so sleep was interrupted hourly by the clump of hobnailed boots along the wooden floors of the hallway. It was annoying, but like everything else we got used to it and paid little attention. The routine was varied by random shakedown inspections, searches for contraband that might have been brought in by the dock detail, always without result. The possessors of such items were too clever at concealment to get caught, and the failure to turn up illegal items so irritated the guards that they resorted to minor brutality on anyone who might be in their way at the time. Even so, it was nothing like we had undergone many times in the past, and made little impression beyond momentary sympathy for the current victim. There was never enough to eat. I have described the diet so many times that the reader should have it well in mind, rice as the staple with some kind of watery soup. Occasionally at Zentsuji there would be some additive to the soup to give it body. Sometimes it would be fish. When fish was available, there would be seven or eight large ones brought in to the cookhouse. There they would be cut up and put in the soup, heads and all. The only discernable difference was a slight oily taste to the bland broth, with occasional bits of meat floating in each bowl. The heads came through the process virtually unscathed, and were a highly prized delicacy, so much so that we developed a roster for their distribution. When your name came up, you got the fish-head, with all the little tid-bits of flesh and fat it contained, protein needed by all of us. Even more prized was a periodic issue of soy beans, which also found their way into the soup. There were usually enough that such a meal was cause for rejoicing, so much so that Lt. Luther Sherry wrote a poem about it.

Beans for Breakfast

I've wracked my brains from morn til' night
For phrases that strike my fancy right
But none can give me such delight
As "Beans for Breakfast"

"Louis for lunch" fair leaves me cold
And plain green soup gets dog-gone old
But the sweetest one that I've been told
Is Beans for Breakfast

Gravy for supper is not too bad
And noodle soup never makes me sad
But if you would make me really glad
Say "Beans for Breakfast"

Beefburgers now I seldom hear
Rabbit tonight is full of cheer
But to me the term most dear
Is Beans for Breakfast

Sukiyaki makes an A-1 diet
Spuds in the soup, OK, just try it
But the dish that almost starts a riot
Is Beans for Breakfast

Corned beef in the rice—a phrase divine
Mangoes or doughnuts would make me shine
But the choice I make 'most every time
Is Beans for Breakfast

Milk just came in; that sounds all right
"Burned rice comin' up"—my face grows light
Still, there's one makes me dream all night
It's "Beans for Breakfast"

At Zentsuji, there was one Red Cross parcel per man issued every two or three months, a good supplement to the usual food and one which gave us just enough additional to minimize the horrors of beri-beri. The extra food was used sparingly as a day-by-day additive to the normal diet, and was extended for as long as possible. The non-smokers used the cigarettes as trading material and the smokers consumed theirs as carefully as they did the food. I made a cigarette holder out of two narrow shoots of bamboo. Then I cut each cigarette into four pieces of equal length, inserted each piece into the holder and smoked it until no paper was visible. I carefully extracted the quarter-inch or so remaining in the holder to put in a small can, then when I had collected enough for a pipeful, smoked it in my bamboo pipe. It would probably have been easier to quit entirely, but there were so few diversions available that I treasured each one, unhealthy or not.

We also received some mail. It was censored by our side to assure there were no military secrets and by the Japanese to obscure their losses. The shortened letters remaining said little but they did let us know that our families were finally aware we were among the living. That must have been a prodigious relief, replacing the uncertainty of the past two years. Information from homes we had almost despaired of seeing again was very good for us too, even though there were a few "Dear John" notes included in the bundles. In late 1944, each prisoner of war in the camp was allowed to record a fifty word message for short-wave broadcast to the States. We knew they would be used for propaganda purposes and had no idea whether they would be received or not, but made the recordings anyway. I found after the war that those propaganda broadcasts were monitored by a large number of amateur radio operators, who recorded the messages and relayed them to our families. It was a much-appreciated public service, and my father had a file two inches thick of recordings and transcripts that had been sent to him by "hams" from all over our country. They had taken the time to monitor Japanese radio broadcasts, and when these messages came over the air, they shared. I'm sure other families had the same experience, and were deeply grateful for it.

The frustration by doctors over the lack of supplies wasn't much different at Zentsuji, but from time to time some medicines were made available, and on rare occasions our doctors were allowed to do something more than cluck sympathetically. One night before dawn in the winter of 1944-45 my friend Jim Baldwin developed severe abdominal pains, waking the whole section with his moans and threshing. We called on Dr. Van Peenan for help and he diagnosed the trouble as a "convovulus," in which part of the intestine gets tied in a knot so that no material can pass through. Dr. Van Peenan said that immediate surgery was the only way to avoid very serious infection and he went to the Japanese for anesthetic and a place to work. They grudgingly gave him a small supply of ether, but told him he would have to find his own operating theater. He went outside and set up an operating table—a door mounted on two saw horses —under one of the large trees in the yard. Father John Wilson, a Catholic chaplain, acted as the anesthetist and the doctor proceeded with the operation using a small pocket kit of instruments he had been able to save. Clean blankets were used to cover the patient, but otherwise there was no antiseptic, except a little alcohol rubbed on Jim's abdomen after the hair had been shaved off with my dull razor. Dr. Van Peenan was skillful; he completed the operation in less than an hour and Jim recovered fully. A minimum of medicine, some improvisation and the doctor's skill saved his life.

Life continued thus until the spring of 1945: read, talk, walk in the yard, farm and try to outwit our captors. There was an abrupt change one morning in the middle of March as we were standing in the *tenko* formation. We heard the rumble of engines overhead unlike the sound of any Japanese plane we knew. It came from a huge silvery bird flying at about thirty thousand feet and headed north toward Honshu. Immediately, the Japanese broke up the formation and ordered us back to our rooms. The blackout curtains were closed tightly and we were told not to look out under any circumstances. We could hear them calling back and forth to each other the works ''*Be ni-ju ku! Be ni-ju ku!*'' I recognized this as ''B-29!'' and knew they must be referring to the new American bomber we had heard about from their newspapers. They were highly disturbed, and didn't seem to know quite what to do ex-

Tom and Dick comparing notes

cept to get us out of the way. Their fears were well-founded: That B-29 was a reconnaisance ''pathfinder'' which preceded the low altitude flight of more than two hundred and fifty of those big birds that roared over our camp just before noon. It turned out they were on their way to make the first large-scale bombing raid on the Japanese mainland during the war. No power on earth could have kept us from peeking out through the curtains to see that magnificent sight: groups of three, nine and sometimes fifteen planes at a time passed overhead and circled until a huge armada had formed before going on to its target. This time they were after Osaka, but it was the first of many raids during the next couple of months that laid waste to Tokyo, Osaka, Kobe, Yokohama and several other of Japan's large cities and industrial centers. We knew, with certainty, that it could not be much longer before we were free and the euphoria produced by those planes is beyond my power to describe. None of our normal activities took place for the rest of that day, but our babbling must have been audible for half a mile. Our jailers took a very dim view of this, but there was little they could do to stop it and they didn't even try. An interesting insight on this day came after the war was over when my younger brother Dick and I were comparing notes. He was a pilot flying B-29s out of Tinian at that time, and had been part of the armada we saw. Their practice was to fly from their base singly or in small groups, forming up over some rendezvous point near Japan before proceeding to the selected target area. Shikoku was convenient for the purpose and was used many times, and if I had known he was up there so close, I would not have been able to contain myself.

For us there was a bad side to this new development. The raids did a great deal of damage throughout Japan, and with each one our relationship with the administration and the guards deteriorated a little more. They cut our rations, curtailed our privileges and the guards became more violent. The atmosphere grew tense and finally we were informed that many of us would be moved to another camp on the main island. The move occurred in May, when four hundred of us were sent north to a countryside location close to the city of Fukui, which was not far from Kyoto. It was called Rokuroshi, and was to be our last stopping place prior to the end of the war.

16

End of the Line

My memories of daily life at Rokuroshi are dim, mostly because we were there only a few months and time to form lasting impressions was limited. The camp contained a single low building surrounded by fencing, which was located about halfway up a sloping hillside. The interior was open except for a small room at one end and sleeping bays occupied both long walls, separated by a passageway extending the length of the barracks. Barred windows provided light and ventilation. In a separate small structure was the *benjo* and shower room, and near it was a washrack just like the one at Zentsuji. A short distance downhill from the compound was a small pond, off-limits to the prisoners, and still lower was the camp headquarters and guardhouse. The surrounding area was partially wooded and there was no evidence of other human habitation to be seen.

Our trip to the camp had been an eye-opener. We went by ferry from Shikoku to Honshu and landed at the port of Moji. The train trip from there to Fukui was one of the most depressing experiences I can remember. Our route took us through the cities of Osaka and Kobe, which had been bustling and vital when I first saw them and were now scenes of total devastation. The bombers had done their job well; as far as I could see the houses and other structures were obliterated. Nothing was left but ashes and occasionally, the twisted steel girders of a burned building or a partially demolished concrete shell. The pattern of streets was there, but there was no traffic, and the few people visible were wandering through the debris in a desultory way looking for anything salvageable and not having much luck. One poignant scene was a man trying to open a charred steel safe, the only remnant left of a once thriving business. Those lonely people were suffering from the lethargy that follows overwhelming shock. I was familiar with that sensation and sympathized with them even though they were the enemy, whom I had no reason to love. What if it had been Seattle, San Francisco or Los Angeles?

Beyond the rubble of the cities, the countryside appeared to be undamaged and the small agricultural villages we passed were picturesque, showing little visual evidence that a war was in progress. Our train elicited no reaction from the townspeople. Its destination city, Fukui, had not yet been a target, probably because it was relatively small and lightly industrialized. We didn't see much of it because immediately after unloading we were formed into a column and began the walk to Rokuroshi, about four miles to the south. We marched without incident along narrow dirt roads, passing through only one little hamlet. The people we saw were neither friendly nor inimical—just disinterested. There were other concerns far more important to them than the sight of barbarians enroute to a prison.

When we arrived at Rokuroshi we became farmers once more. The conditions were similar to Zentsuji, and we had a fairly large plot to cultivate on the hillside adjacent to the camp. Again the soil was rocky and the methods used to tame it familiar, but there was one difference. After the field was prepared and the vegetables planted, we not only irrigated by hand with water from the pond but added nightsoil for fertilizer. Nightsoil is human waste, collected by the "honey-dipper," our name for the ox-cart driver whose job was to empty out the *benjo* pits periodically. His simple equipment was a long narrow two-wheeled cart carrying a row of wooden barrels, always either seven or nine of them. He would clean out the hole using a long-handled dipper and then trundle away with the mess. We had seen this operation many times before and had never thought much about what happened to the waste after that, but now we found out. The barrels were emptied into a pit about eight feet square and five feet deep, until it was half full. Then water was added to fill and the whole concoction allowed to ferment for several days, until it was ready for use. Wood buckets were then filled and carried on a neck-yoke to the field where a small quantity was dipped out for each plant. Nobody fought for the fertilizing assignment, but we all had to do it. At first, all the soap we could find could not make us feel clean afterwards, but one can get used to anything. The results were spectacular: all the vegetables were tremendous. White radishes (*daikon*) twenty inches long and four inches in diameter were common. We never had to eat our own produce grown this way because, as in the past, it was either taken away or hadn't matured by the time we left in September. Although our revulsion was instinctive, we had lived on that same kind of stuff for years with no discernible ill effects, so I guess it was okay. Certainly the Japanese were strong and healthy, and food grown this way had been their diet forever.

Except for farming, life here was unlike life at Zentsuji. Both the quantity and quality of food issues were drastically reduced, and as the months passed the effects of that reduction became increasingly visible. Everyone lost weight and dietary deficiency diseases began to reappear, not as bad as they had been in Yodogawa but still serious. The lack of food was such an important part of our daily existence that any other consideration became minor, even rigid controls and their accompanying brutality. The guards, egged on by the administration, seemed to delight in making life miserable and used any excuse to become violent. Looking back, I suppose much of their hatred was the result of severe damage to Japan by our air raids and the realization that their war was lost. Like children, they lashed out at the closest available objects of scorn, which were their captives.

The senior American officer, Colonel Unruh, was the prisoner commander and the conduit through which Japanese orders were transmitted. It was the usual practice for his Japanese counterpart to step out of headquarters and bellow, "Unruh!" He was then expected to sprint down the hill to receive the orders. The procedure was unmilitary as well as uncivil, and was humiliating to all of us. So, it was a real surprise to have the senior Japanese officer come to the barracks building about September 1, 1945, and quietly request to speak with Col. Unruh. At the Colonel's invitation he entered the small room at the end of the building and shut the door. We knew something was up, but were not prepared for the statement Col. Unruh made at the end of their brief meeting. He opened the door, stepped out, asked for attention then announced without preamble, "The War is Ended." The barracks erupted in a volcano of noise and it took a long while for it to subside sufficiently that he could deliver the balance of the message. My hysteria was typical. I laughed and cried at the same time, shouted obscenities and uttered threats against the guard force. There were also prayers of thanksgiving. When things calmed down a little, Unruh continued. Now we were all ears, not wanting to miss a single word.

The gist of it was that an unconditional surrender by the Japanese had been signed about two weeks earlier. We were to stay where we were and remain patient until repatriation teams could get to us. Though supplies were short, the Japanese would feed us as well as possible. The American air force would make a food drop by parachute in the camp area as soon as they were apprised of our exact location. We were to fashion a large white cross on the roof to help them identify it as a POW camp. We would be free to roam the countryside, but were asked to be restrained in our actions toward civilians. After giving these few instructions, the camp commander left the building, bowing low to the Colonel before he left. It was the first such courtesy shown to any of us in three and a half years.

In our barracks the noise and jubilation resumed and the celebration continued without abatement, beyond my ability to describe it. The memory of brutality from the guards was so fresh in our minds that a few were bitter enough to attempt immediate retaliation. Someone suggested it and the cry was taken up by others, until a group formed and stormed down to headquarters to begin their vengeance. There was nobody there, guards and weapons had disappeared. It was just as well, there could have been violence that would have haunted those men for a long time to come, despite the fact that all of us had experienced worse.

In the meantime, the rest of us set out to obliterate any evidence that this had been a prison. The bars were torn from the windows and the fences disappeared in a matter of minutes. Ladders were cobbled together from the posts so that we could climb to the roof and make the white cross. Anything available of light color was used: sheets, blankets, undershirts, towels and cloth scrounged from headquarters. When we were finished, there was a large cross on each slope of the gabled roof. We had to go up the hill a fair distance to see what one of them looked like, and it was beautiful. All those scraps held down by rocks from our garden wall made a very effective signal to the airplanes. We expected them that afternoon; of course they didn't come—the military does not work that fast.

Our elation continued through the night, reinforced by the first delivery of the promised supplies from the Japanese, a very large drum of sake, Nipponese rice wine. About half of the four hundred men there were in no condition to partake. I was in the other half, and we went on the grandaddy of all benders. We drank the stuff by the canteen cupful (more than a pint) paying no heed to the dribbling down our chins and shirt-fronts. After three or four of these big belts, Hap Armold, Ben Riall and I decided to go exploring down the hill and through the forest. It was a raucous group, which sang off-key and shouted just to hear the echo. We got lost, but finally came across an isolated house where the occupants allowed us to enter and politely welcomed us. We didn't realize it, but they were probably scared to death of what we might do. I used my rusty Nippon-go to bargain for more sake which we needed like a second head, and some carved wooden frogs I wanted for souveniers. At the end and after much palaver, our hosts guided us back to the camp, all three much the worse for wear. I decided I needed a bath and jumped into the pond. The only problem was that I forgot to take off my shoes or clothing and my friends told me I nearly drowned, but I don't remember that. In fact, I remember nothing more until the next morning, when I woke from a peaceful sleep in the drain trough of our soap-slick wash rack. The waking was sudden, caused by some impatient soul who opened one of the cold water taps into my face. I came up fast, banging my head on the tap in the process, and rolled off the rack onto the duckboards below. My head felt twice the size of a basketball, but I got no sympathy from anyone. Most of the ambulatory men were in similar condition anyway. It took a full day and the next night to return to normal, and I have been cautious about sake ever since. It had been a great party.

The airplanes we expected did not come that day or for three days after, and we began to get concerned because we were running out of food and nothing beyond the sake had been delivered by the Japanese. Col. Unruh finally dispatched a man to Kyoto (Fukui had been bombed a few weeks earlier) to try and make contact with our people. His mission was successful, and early the following morning one of those beautiful B-29's flew over, so low I thought we'd lose the roof. He had not missed seeing the crosses, and made a turn and another low pass, then repeated before disappearing off to the south.

Three or four hours after that first pass, we heard the now familiar rumble of multi-engined aircraft coming toward us. Four of them overflew the camp, then made a turn somewhere north of the hillcrest and came roaring back about eight hundred feet above the ground, one set of bomb-bay doors open on each plane. Suddenly, instead of bombs large pallets were released from the bays, and parachutes of all colors blossomed above them. Many dropped in the camp area, others a short distance away and a few drifted as much as a mile from us. The planes made another pass and dropped a second load with about the same results, then wiggled their wings and departed. It was a beautiful scene: flowers floating down from the sky bearing crates, bundles and barrels—manna from Heaven. They contained all sorts of things: such as canned and packaged foods, GI chocolate and Baby Ruth candy bars, clothing, shoes, dried milk, cigarettes and current news magazines including the overseas edition of Time and Newsweek. Most reached the ground undamaged, but there were a few spectacular failures. I remember one of those vividly. Someone had welded together two fifty-five gallon drums end to end, then filled one side with chocolate and the other with milk. The chutes failed to open, so those heavy drums made a crater in the ground nearly six feet deep. Of course they ruptured, creating the only chocolate swimming pool I ever saw. There was enough other stuff that we really didn't miss that cocoa.

We were also concerned about the parachutes that had drifted far away and were afraid they had been lost forever. We worried needlessly because each package had a placard on it written in *Kanji,* containing dire threats to anyone who diverted the contents away from the prisoners. The natives believed those threats and soon ox-carts arrived, bearing the stray bundles for us. It had been quite a day. There was more than enough good, solid American food to feed all four hundred of us for at least two weeks, including such things as canned meat, dried potatoes, vegetables and staples we had not seen for years. At first it was every man for himself, and all of us had the opportunity to gorge to his heart's content. I dined on corned beef and chocolate bars, and ate so many of the latter they made me sick, and for a long time afterward the smell of chocolate caused an automatic stomach upset. After a while reason prevailed, and the foodstuffs were collected together so they could be cooked in the mess hall and shared equally by everyone. The extra food had come just in time to save the lives of many and enable the rest to begin our physical rehabilitation.

Though the clothing was welcome it wasn't important because it was still summer and what we had was marginally adequate. The GI shoes, however, were a godsend. We had been walking around on *geta* for so long we hardly remembered anything else. For the first time feet were both comfortable and warm. But, after the gorging and outfitting were over, the most satisfactory items of all were the magazines. For the first time we learned about the atomic bombs that ended the war quickly. Although they cost so many Japanese lives, they saved ours. We knew there were standing orders that all prisoners of war were to be liquidated at the first invasion attempt by our side. It had not been a cheerful prospect, akin to what a condemned man feels after his appeal has been rejected. The bomb eliminated the invasion and that threat.

This was not the only news that warmed us. We got a glimpse of wartime America and the public support given the armed forces. The leggy pictures of Betty Grable and the other pin-up gals were displayed. We chuckled at the stories of the rationing and shortages that were under-

SCENES AT ROKUROSHI PRIOR TO DEPARTURE

Enjoying the good stuff from the B-29's

The barracks

Fred Garrett with
his new crutches

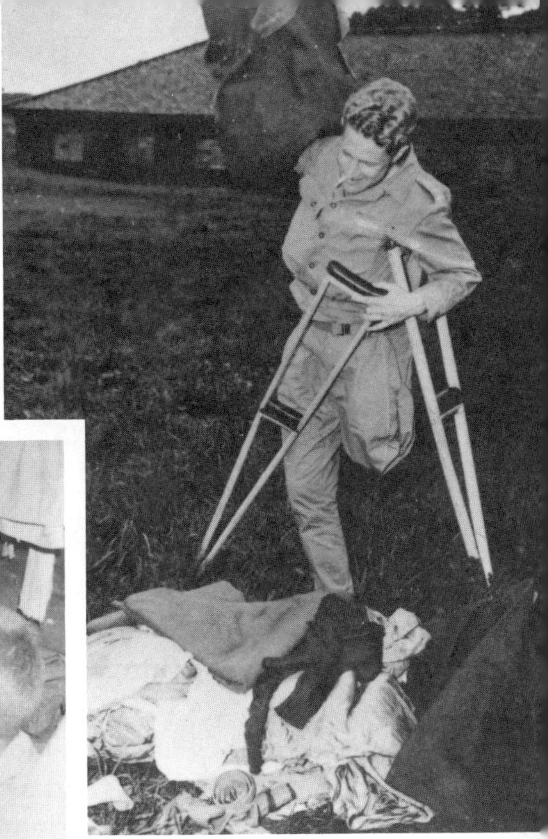

What will home be like?

Horseplay with the recovery team.
Yoder, Boyt and Powell in center.

gone by the civilian population: limited gasoline, having to wait for enough coupons to buy meat, no silk stockings for the ladies, short liquor supplies. It was heartening to see how bravely people had withstood those hardships, particularly since we had been living in the lap of luxury for so long. Other news was not so amusing, with its summaries of the battles for Okinawa and Iwo Jima, Guam and Tinian, Leyte Gulf and Rabaul. Those articles made me realize that we were not the only ones to suffer in that war, and that we were lucky to be alive. We had focused on our own troubles almost exclusively, and the reading helped us put things in perspective.

After the excitement and frenetic activity following that dramatic announcement of war's ending and the subsequent air drop of food and supplies, it was hard to wait patiently for the repatriation teams to arrive. Eventually they did, nearly a month after the signing of the surrender documents. There were several in the party which rolled into camp in two GI trucks. Two were doctors and two were nurses, and the rest were records personnel who had to identify each of us so that information about our welfare could be transmitted to the Army and to our families. The medical team concentrated on the bedridden and did a lot of good during the day and a half it took to complete these records. Ironically, we were concerned about the people on the team. They all had sallow, yellow complexions and we thought they must have contracted some obscure tropical disease. It turned out that the yellow tinge was caused by atabrine, which was issued to all troops in the Pacific as prophylaxis against malaria. It may have been effective but it certainly hadn't made those people look any better.

Eventually the classification and treatment were completed and three days after the team arrived we were moved from the camp, walking or riding (for the sick ones) to Fukui, then traveling by train to Yokohama. The train ride into Yokohama was uneventful except for the increasing tension arising from expectation of things to come. We hadn't realized how important we had become to our country, and so were unprepared for the impressive reception that awaited us in the railroad station in Yokohama. There were two batallions of infantry lined up, resplendent in stiffly starched uniforms, gleaming helmets and highly polished boots. They were called to a rigid "present arms" as we began to exit the train and remained so until the last man disembarked. There was a full band playing familiar martial airs that brought a king-sized lump to my throat. Our seedy-looking group lined up in a loose formation (most of us had forgotten our military habits) and endured a mercifully short welcoming speech from General Robert Eichelberger, commander of the Eighth Army, followed by another equally short from General Kreuger, commander of the Sixth Army. Both were famous soldiers whose names we recognized from our clandestine newspapers at Zentsuji, and we were flattered that they would take the time to welcome us home. Both of them either saluted each of us or shook our hands as we climbed aboard the trucks that were to take us to the dock. I think they were all afraid we might try to vent the bitterness we felt toward the Japanese by some acts of retaliation if allowed to remain in the city. They prevented that by transporting us directly to the ship that was to take us on the first leg of our journey home. We didn't care; we were too eager to get going.

17

Homeward Bound

AP-171 was the large grey troop transport that had been assigned to carry ex prisoners of war (what a great word—''ex'') home. It was berthed in the harbor at Yokusuka, the largest of the naval bases, and was prepared for us. As we went through the entry port, we were instructed to get rid of all but personal mementos: musette bags by now tattered and torn, clothing, shoes, old blankets or anything else that could possibly be contaminated. We went through a hot shower followed by a de-lousing procedure, and then to the supply section for new issues of everything from the skin out. It was a great luxury to have clothing that fitted. Even though it was GI khaki, I felt as though it had been cut by Brooks Brothers. There was real toothpaste, shaving cream and a new Gillette safety razor with a whole package of extra blades. To be able to have a clean, painless, close shave was sheer bliss, rivaled by the application of copious quantities of after-shave lotion to tingling skin. At last, I knew I was on the way home.

The ship had a section that had been prepared for hospital use, and those who needed treatment were assigned there. The rest of us were placed in troop compartments. Navy personnel apologized for what they thought were very crowded conditions, but we considered them luxurious, especially since we were to be allowed the run of the vessel. Everyone in the crew seemed anxious to make our voyage as pleasant as possible, which was a dramatic change from the XX *Maru.* We remained tied up at the dock for the balance of that first day while the medical staff began its routine of physical examinations for all of us, giving special attention to the occupants of the sick-bay. Huge quantities of well-cooked Navy chow were provided in the mess-hall at almost any hour. I was disturbed to discover that my stomach had shrunk. I could not possibly put away a full meal at one time and would have to eat only small amounts at short intervals to maintain an adequate diet. To some degree that condition still persists, which is probably a good thing since it is one means of weight control.

Early the next morning, we untied and pulled away from the dock destined for Manila. We were to spend a few days there and then head for San Francisco via Honolulu. It was a beautiful day, so clear we could see everything. What a sight it was, there were ships everywhere around us all the way to the horizon: aircraft carriers, battleships, cruisers, transports, destroyers and many others whose function could only be guessed. There must have been fifteen hundred of them. I remarked to one of the naval lieutenents that the entire Navy must have been collected there to celebrate the fall of Japan. He scoffed at that and said this was only a task force and there were others scattered all over the world. What a difference from the months immediately following Pearl Harbor! There were all kinds of airplanes flying, from the smallest observation craft to the largest multi-engined bomber. I remember particularly a Catalina patrol amphibian because it flew low and just off our port bow. The hatch facing us was open and an airman leaning against the coaming with his legs crossed gave a negligent wave as they passed. I hadn't seen this kind of nonchalance for so long it left a lasting impression, and lasting impressions were the order of the day—everything was new and exciting. This helped to assuage the disappointment of not flying home. That had been the original plan, but a typhoon a few days before had damaged installations and planes so much that an airlift became impossible. Flying to the States would have been a great way to end the war, but it was probably just as well it didn't happen. The weeks of good food I had on the slower sea voyage, which took a month and a half, did much to restore the weight I had lost and I arrived in San Francisco looking nearly the same as when I left four and a half years earlier.

We settled down to the ship's routine very easily: eat, sleep, eat, walk the deck, eat, play cards. I slept on deck most of the time because the weather was nice and I didn't like to be cooped up below. We passed by Formosa on the way to the Philippines but did not stop. I liked that because the few memories I had of it were most unpleasant. Arrival in Manila Bay was a shock. Corregidor was still barren, though there was evidence that vegetation was beginning to return, and Bataan seemed untouched. Sunken ships dotted the harbour near the Port Area, which was a shambles, as was much of Manila itself. The Japanese had fought for every inch of the city, dynamiting and destroying behind them everything not already damaged by our side. It was sad to see that once-beautiful metropolis in ruins, but it was not as bad, I suppose, as what had happened to Osaka and Kobe. My feelings about the destruction, however, were much different. I had regretted their demolition on an intellectual basis as part of the fortunes of war. Here, the reaction was emotional and my smoldering anger at the Japanese flared anew. After all, we had tried to leave it an undamaged open city when forced to depart, and they could have done the same.

We transferred off the ship and moved to a temporary replacement center about five or six miles west of Manila. It was a tent city, specifically created to process returning prisoners. There our records were brought up to date and we received part of the back pay that had been accruing since the war started. In addition, we underwent careful medical exams and were injected with booster shots against tropical disease. Most important to us, we had been promoted; I became a Captain and everybody else advanced one rank. The officers were issued brand new uniforms: gabardine Eisenhower jackets and pink trousers, with all the appropriate insignia and service ribbons. We became officers and gentlemen once more, and just wearing that uniform did much to restore the esprit that had been missing for so long. People had been collected there from camps all over the war zone, in Japan, Manchuria and Formosa, and the pure pleasure of seeing old friends again is indescribable. Among them was Col. Mallonee, who had spent most of the time since O'Donnell in Manchuria. He was in good shape and had acquired a bottle of stateside Three Feathers whiskey which we killed in one afternoon while bringing each other up to date. It tasted like nectar to both of us, and I determined to acquire a case when we finally reached San Francisco. He gave me the bad news that Bonner, Savoie and Hendry were all dead, and we offered them a silent toast. Mallonee's life had been little better than mine. He had gone from O'Donnell to Formosa for a few months, then to Manchuria for the balance of the war. Their camp had been liberated by the Russians shortly after the bomb fell, and he had come to Manila by a very circuitous route. I was happy to find we were to go to the States on the same ship within the next few days. It was a sweet/sour reunion. From others I also heard about the fate of additional friends. Reed Shurtleff had died of cerebral malaria in Cabanatuan and George Armantrout had gone down on the Oryoko Maru. Wayne Fisher, I knew, had died at O'Donnell. Bill Smith and Gene Holmes had stayed at Cabanatuan, were liberated by the famous Ranger raid and were already back in the States. When last heard of, Chuck Francis had been in a camp near Mukden. The list went on.

I knew I would be seeing Reed's parents before long and wanted to obtain for them information about how he died and where he was buried. Scouting the area near the depot area, I ran into a field artillery outfit with a couple of Cessna-built observation aircraft. I determined to borrow one and conned a pilot into taking me to Cabanatuan. It was easy to do because he was bored to death and wanted to get some more flying time. We made arrangements to take off early the next morning, fly up there and return in the afternoon. Once airborne, he solemnly informed me that regulations required we fly at five thousand feet over Manila Bay, and we climbed to that altitude, but there was a British carrier in the bay and he was curious about it, so we dived on it and buzzed. The commotion our actions caused on the deck of that carrier was clearly visible, and didn't stop with our passing. We learned later the English were ready to shoot at us, but decided to press for a court martial instead. It was fortunate for the pilot that they could not identify either the plane or its base (he did not answer radio calls), but they did cause a lot of trouble for American headquarters in spite of that. Now that we were close to the surface, my new buddy declared, ''What the Hell, we are already down here, might as well stay.'' We did stay low, never flying more than fifty feet above the surface for the rest of the time, raising one wing-tip or the other to clear the occasional tall tree that got in our way. But we got to Cabanatuan safely, landed on the road and taxied into the parking lot next to the graves registration office. Those people were gracious about helping me and I got the information I needed. They even took me to Reed's grave, and that one excursion was plenty. I had already seen enough of Cabanatuan to last a lifetime and had no further desire to explore. So we returned the way we had come, right on the deck because that pilot must have been afraid of heights. This time though, he let me operate the controls most of the way. It was surprisingly easy and I had a ball.

In about ten days, our processing was complete and we were given sudden orders to rejoin the ship. They caught many unprepared: I and three others had borrowed a Jeep for an exploration run into Manila. We browsed around there for a while, had a beer or two and went back to camp, to find our friends had deserted it. It didn't take long to find out that they had departed an hour before, taking their baggage with them. The chances of catching up were slim, but we couldn't face another few weeks delay, so threw our stuff together, dragooned a driver and took off for the port area. It must have made quite a spectacle; four of us, four big barracks bags and a driver hightailing it along those narrow roads in an open Jeep. We made little noise except for the horn, but we didn't need to: that speeding, sadly overloaded vehicle made all the statement necessary.

We passed through security, skidded onto the dock, piled off and rushed up the gang-plank minutes before it was raised. In the flurry of departure preparation, our driver was called into one of the offices to "make a report," and on his return found his Jeep had disappeared. He raised a lot of hell to no avail; none of the sailors on the dock had seen a thing. But we had. As soon as his back was turned, a cargo boom swung out from our deck, hooked to a hastily prepared sling and the jeep was aboard and in the hold in less time than it takes to tell it. In short order, it was repainted grey and the Navy had new transportation at low cost, as neat a con job as I ever saw. The ship already had two others, no doubt acquired the same way. The stunt was probably instigated by a Chief Petty Officer, and I'm sure it was accomplished with the tacit approval of the Skipper. The driver faced reams of paper work and some disciplinary action, but they didn't care about that.

We were given royal treatment from the time the recovery team arrived at Rokuroshi, but also had been subjected to much questioning. Some of it had been official, but a good deal was prompted by sheer curiosity. Although well meant, the questioning had served to keep my painful memories alive, constantly renewing the rage and hate I felt against the Japanese. I knew this was not healthy. If it were not controlled it could warp my entire outlook on life and prevent a normal readjustment to freedom and responsibility. All those around me, as well as myself, would feel the adverse effects of that and suffer unnecessarily. Consequently, I resolved to put it behind me and to forget, if possible, those difficult and trying years. I would look forward instead of back, and begin the next phase of my life unencumbered by a burden of hatred. I thought part of the therapy would have to be closing off the past by refusal to discuss it or to answer disturbing questions concerning it. Having made that decision, which was not an easy one, I could now focus on the future and make plans for it. I would finish the work required for my engineering degree. I hoped there would be marriage and a family and I did not think I wanted a military career. There had been too much regimentation and control already and I needed more freedom of choice than the Army could provide. I discussed these ideas with Col. Mallonee, expecting a professional soldier who had spent his entire adult life in the service to disagree. Oddly enough, he didn't, and instead encouraged me in the path I had chosen, probably realizing my need to break completely away from the traumatic effects of the recent past. Mallonee was a good friend, whose advice and counsel I appreciated.

The stretch from Manila to Honolulu was a repetition of the one we had made in the President Cleveland except there were no nurses to flirt with. We played a lot of poker and talked a lot, mostly about the future. Few people discussed their own feelings, which were private and kept to ourselves, a habit for me that still persists to some degree. I believe most of us were uncertain of how we would be able to adjust to normal living, and were unwilling to share that fear. I was emotional and little things could affect me; one of those was the first long-wave broadcast from the States, which we heard on the wardroom radio. It happened to be the Sunday morning broadcast of the Mormon Tabernacle Choir from Salt Lake City and I had heard it many times before, but this time it was special.

The singing was great music and evoked memories that brought tears to my eyes.

We tied up in Hawaii at the mouth of the narrow entrance to Pearl Harbor. The ship would spend one night there and then sail for San Francisco, and we were all free to do whatever we wanted in the interim. Col. Mallonee and I and a few others decided that we wanted to call home, and went to the overseas telephone office. It was crowded because there were many ex-POW's who had the same idea and at first the operators were not helpful. Apparently there were so many military and civilian personnel stationed in Hawaii making calls that each had to be scheduled several days in advance, eliminating any chance we late-comers might have. Some supervisor, however, realized who we were and where we had been and solicited the co-operation of callers on that night's list. Without hesitation, those good people deferred to us and gave up their places. It was a nice thing to do and none of us will ever forget their generosity. My own call took two hours to complete and waked my family in the early hours of the morning. We were so excited that the conversation was disjointed and almost incoherent, but it was satisfying nonetheless. My father and step-mother agreed to be in San Francisco when we docked on October 19, 1945. After those conversations anything else would have been anticlimax, so we returned to the ship for a sleepless, nostalgic night.

The next morning just before our ship was to leave the dock, we were treated to a stirring parade. Seven battleships and cruisers steamed by the AP-171, in line, on their way out to sea. Crews were mustered on the decks and the bands were playing. They passed very close, and as each ship drew alongside us, its colors were dipped in salute. Those mighty ships were magnificent and their courtesies, together with those of our anonymous benefactors of the night before, made us realize that not only were we home, but were wanted and welcomed. The realization helped to erase some of the bitterness of Bataan; we were no longer bastards.

The days between Hawaii and San Francisco passed uneventfully. As dawn was breaking the morning of October nineteenth, we approached the California coast. There was a patchy fog that would dissipate later with the rising sun, and the mournful notes of our foghorn were necessary to warn off possible collisions. Excitement was rising and everyone wanted to be the first to call out, "There it is!" We were so intent on getting the first view that we nearly missed seeing the submarine rising out of the water alongside. It looked ugly and lethal, but was there to guide us into the harbor through the minefields still in place. The transit was slow and the ship made many turns to negotiate that labyrinth. At length we made it, and two other things happened at about the same time. The fog burned off and the Golden Gate bridge appeared out of the mist, outlined in all its glory by the morning sun rising behind it. We had a saying in Japan, "Golden Gate in Forty-eight," and here we were, three years early! I cannot describe my ecstatic feelings adequately; I just stared, and was not able to speak. All I could do was to gaze at that beautiful bridge and the white buildings on the hills behind it in silent gratitude. I had been determined to make it through, but never truly thought that would be possible. By the grace of God I had returned, and I uttered a fervent prayer of heartfelt thanksgiving for that beneficence.

The lump in my throat disappeared and attention turned to other things as soon as we passed under the bridge. There was a huge electric sign on one of the hills near Fort Mason flashing ''Welcome Home,'' and a flotilla of small boats, a few tugs and a ferryboat assembled to escort us to the dock. They assumed position on our starboard side, and AP-171 took a decided list in that direction because it seemed most of the pretty girls in San Francisco had gathered to greet us. They called, ''Any one aboard from Minnesota?'' Our whole shipload roared. ''Anyone there from Kansas?'' Another roar. ''Any from California?'' Still another roar. We exchanged delighted comments all the way to Pier Seven, until we rounded the end of the pier and slid up alongside. The lines were thrown and secured to the bitts, the slack taken in and motion ceased. We were home at last.

I searched the faces of the crowd on the dock looking for a familiar grouping, and finally picked them out. There was my father, mustache a little greyer than I remembered, my step-mother looking elegant and an Air Force lieutenant who could only have been my younger brother. With them were the Westcotts, a couple who had been close college friends, he resplendent in Navy blues and she waving a scarf. It was good that it took a while to lower the gang-plank because I needed the time to compose myself. Eventually it was my turn to go ashore, barracks bag dragging behind me, to as warm a reception as I could have desired. No one could say much, but eyes were full of tears. We went straight from the dock to the adjacent warehouse where the family car was waiting. It was in that restricted area courtesy of my brother, who had always been an operator, and within minutes we were on our way to the Mark Hopkins hotel, where rooms had been engaged. I dropped my bag in my room and then all of us congregated at the Top of the Mark and the talk began. I put a little damper on it when I refused to say much about Bataan and the prison camps and stuck to my shipboard resolve, but everyone seemed to understand and didn't force the issue. It was a great reunion anyway and lasted the entire afternoon and evening.

The next morning I had to report in to Letterman Hospital for another check-up. It didn't last long, so a couple of friends and I sought out the first liquor store we could find. I asked the proprieter for a bottle of that wonderful Three Feathers I had so enjoyed at the replacement center. He looked at me queerly and asked, "What?" I repeated the order and he was still skeptical, asking "Why would you want that rot-gut?" So I told him the story and he laughed, saying "You have been gone a long time, haven't you?" He refused to sell the Three Feathers and provided two bottles of good bonded bourbon instead, one of them on the house. They smoothed out the afternoon for all of us.

The Westcotts had arranged a date for that evening with another Salt Lake girl living in the City. When I went to pick her up, I was smitten. She was beautiful, dark-haired, smart and warm, and I thought, "This is for me." We had two or three wonderful days together before I had to entrain for Van Nuys Hospital in southern California to undergo another series of tests. On one of those we had dinner at the Palace Hotel, in their elegant and old-fashioned ballroom. My friends Curly Ricks, Mel Rosen and I insisted that the centerpiece be removed and a large bowl of cooked rice be substituted for it, and we used that bowl for an ashtray all evening long. A year before we would have fought over it.

After that interlude, we boarded a southbound hospital train in full uniform. We were in pretty good shape even after the carousing that had been done, so it was a surprise to be ordered to undress and climb into the hospital beds running the full length of the car, each by its own picture window. Then the train rolled, following the Embarcadero from Letterman Hospital to the Bay bridge, then cutting across South San Francisco and down the peninsula from there. For the first stretch crowds lined the tracks, waving handkerchiefs and cheering, and our function was to wave back weakly. It was staged propaganda in its worst form, because as soon as we cleared the City everyone was up and dressed, and we stayed that way for the rest of the trip. Most of us resented the crude charade, but some enjoyed putting on the show.

There would be other disillusionments and frustrations to follow, but good times also. The important fact for us was that the war had ended, prisons and their memories were in the past and a whole lifetime lay ahead.

Epilogue

More than forty years have passed since these events occurred, and the future I wished to protect by silence on the subject is now the past. The purpose of that silence was at least partially achieved, and I was able to concentrate on family and career without much emotional disturbance from the war and its aftermath. However, with the years has come some maturity, the sharpness of those images has faded and discussing them has become less difficult. I am in my seventies instead of my twenties, my wife has suggested many times that my children ought to know something of my wartime background, and I should write about it. Certainly, time was available during retirement, and the implication was that the task should be done before senility arrived. I began the effort three years ago with a certain amount of trepidation, not knowing whether my memory of the experiences would be clear enough to capture or too painful to put on paper. Happily, neither has been a great problem; instead, the writing has been a catharsis, purging my mind of a lot of useless prejudice. I'm glad it was done, and hope my daughter and sons receive insight from reading it commensurate with what I obtained from the writing.

It is 1989 now instead of 1945. I still weigh about the same as then, but it is distributed differently. My forehead is located somewhere near the nape of my neck, joints are creakier, hearing aids are needed and the eyes are not what they used to be. A good drive on the golf course is about one hundred eighty yards where it used to be a muffed shot. Otherwise, I'm as good as I ever was—almost. My life is full. That lovely girl in San Francisco and I were married, and she has provided me with fine children, a daughter and two sons of whom we are very proud. They, in their turn, are producing grandchildren for us to spoil, which we do at the slightest provocation.

But I miss the association with men who shared the Japanese experience with me. They have scattered across the country, living in small towns and large cities in almost every state, so it is difficult to keep in touch. Chuck Francis retired from the Army and lives in Clear Lake, California. Bill Smith the same, but is living in Oceanside. Bob Silhavy has a home in Coeur d'Alene, Idaho and Gene Boyt in Chickasha, Oklahoma. Norm Wides lives in Kentucky, Bill Adair in Dallas and Fred Wildish in Seattle. Ralph Yoder is a successful businessman in St. Louis. There is an organization called American Defenders of Bataan and Corregidor that tries to keep these people together by means of regional and national conventions each year. I am a member of that, but have not been able to be as active as I would like. Instead I rely on their publication, the "Quan." There is also a quarterly newsletter issued as a labor of love to those connected with Zentsuji, by Kermit Lay and his good wife, Paula. They live in the San Francisco Bay area, have published it for years and have become the cement that has held many of the ex-

POW's together. The letter contains news about Zentsujians from all parts of our country and also some from those in Australia and England who were there. The only trouble with it is that its necrology section grows longer with each issue. I hope they know how much pleasure their efforts have given us all.